D0856579

DISCARDED BY
MT LEBANON LIBRARY

5

a day

soups

5

a day

soups

Anastasia Argent

soupologie

Photography by Tamin Jones

KYLE BOOKS

Mt. Lebanon Public Library
16 Castle Shannon Blvd
Pittsburgh, PA 15228-2252
412-531-1912 | www.mtlebanonlibrary.org

CONTENTS

Introduction

We all know we should be eating more fruit and vegetables. One of the most common pieces of advice is that we should aim to eat at least five portions of fruit and vegetables a day, recommended by the World Health Organization (WHO).

Despite the fact that most of us know we should eat more healthily, we often fall short. A couple of years ago, we (a family team with a love for creating plant-based recipes) decided to develop a range of soups, with each one providing all of the recommended 5 a day. What could be better than eating a pot of soup and knowing that, with almost no effort, you've hit your 5 a day goal?

While creating those soups, we discovered that the regulations surrounding 5 a day are not exactly straightforward. As a result, it took us over a year to develop the range, and we learned many startling food and nutritional facts along the way. All the WHO rules and regulations made sense once we saw the unprecedented quantity of vitamins and minerals we can get from eating this wide variety of fruits and vegetables every day.

People don't think twice about popping a multivitamin pill or taking supplements on a daily basis to rectify potential deficiencies in their diets. However, the nutritional benefits of eating the correct food in the first place can considerably reduce the need for these supplements. We've included a nutritional breakdown for every recipe so that you can see for yourselves just how super-charged with goodness each one is!

It's easy to fall into the trap of viewing healthy food as tasteless and boring, while seeing unhealthy food as a guilty pleasure. That's why, in this book, we have tried to create recipes that have all the benefits of healthy eating without compromising on flavour. We had a lot of fun developing these delicious and nutritious soups and meals, and we're sure you'll love making – and eating – them! We hope that by pouring everything we've learned into exciting recipes, and throwing in some surprising foodie facts, you'll easily smash your 5 a day and enjoy yourselves at the same time.

Anastasia & the Soupologie team

What makes up our 5 a day?

The majority of us are not even coming close to the 5 a day target. Although most people know about the 5 a day guidelines and understand that they need to be eating more fruit and vegetables, very few people are aware of what the exact recommendations are.

The basic guidelines are as follows:

- **80g (2¾oz) fresh or frozen whole fruits and vegetables = 1 portion**
  Doubling up on one type of fruit or vegetable, or even two types from the same plant family, will still only count as a single portion. This is because WHO guidelines state that variety is important, and that we need to consume a diverse selection of fruits and vegetables. Work on the basis that variety is the spice of life. If you happen to have 80g (2¾oz) leeks and 80g (2¾oz) onions in one dish, that will only count as having had one portion of your 5 a day, as leeks and onions both come from the Allium genus of vegetables, which also includes garlic.
- **30g (1oz) dried fruit, such as apricots, prunes or sultanas = 1 portion**
  Ideally you should only have one portion of dried fruit a day due to its high sugar content.
- **40g (1¼oz) vegetable concentrate or 20g (¾oz) double concentrate = 1 portion**
- **150ml (¼ pint) fruit juice or vegetable juice = 1 portion**
  As with the 80g (2¾oz) portion guidelines, doubling up the amount of juice or even having a portion of fruit juice and a portion of vegetable juice will still only count as one portion. Juicing might seem like a quick fix to help you reach your 5 a day, but when fruits and vegetables are blitzed into juice, a lot of the fabulous fibre (which is needed to help slow down sugar absorption in our blood) is extracted and tossed aside in the juicing process. We should also be wary of shop-bought juices with added sugars and sweeteners. Again, only 150ml (¼ pint) counts, and often shop-bought juices come in larger bottles. This means that we fill ourselves with a lot of sugary juice rather than the whole fruit, missing out on the pulp and fibre.
- **80g (2¾oz) canned fruit or vegetables = 1 portion**
  When opting for canned goods, it is best to pick foods in their natural juice, or water, preferably with no added sugar or salt.
- **80g (2¾oz) beans or pulses = 1 portion**
  This includes soya beans. As above, only one portion of beans or pulses counts towards your 5 a day. If you eat 80g (2¾oz) beans and 80g (2¾oz) pulses, that will count as one portion.

What doesn't count towards your 5 a day?

- Seeds
- Grains
- Nuts
- Coconut
- White potatoes (despite having many nutritional benefits, white potatoes are classified as the carbohydrate part of a meal, rather like rice, pasta or noodles)
- Yams
- Cassava
- Plantain

While the foods listed above do not count as part of your 5 a day, they have many nutritional benefits and should therefore still be enjoyed as part of a healthy diet. In fact, you can easily incorporate them as an add-on to our 5 a day soups: grains and seeds pair nicely with most soups; potatoes naturally make a great accompaniment to many recipes and coconuts work well to make dishes mild and creamy.

5 a day for kids

We're hoping that this cookbook will help you and the people around you lead a healthier lifestyle. 82 per cent of children aged 5 to 15 were not meeting the recommended guidelines in 2018 – this could be remedied by making eating 5 a day feel more achievable, accessible and, most importantly, fun! The recipes in this book are designed to make healthy eating something that you look forward to rather than something that feels like a chore.

If you'd like to encourage little ones to enjoy getting their 5 a day alongside you, this cookbook is a great place to start. Teaching children about the importance of fruit and vegetables at an early age is a great way to promote healthy eating habits as they head into adulthood. To get kids involved, why not encourage them to pick out fruit and vegetables incorporating each colour of the rainbow? That way you'll be giving the next generation of 'foodies' a helping hand by teaching them the benefits of healthy eating and the ease with which you can reach your 5 a day.

Why 5 a day?

We are at our best when we have great fuel to keep us going, and fruit and vegetables are integral to maintaining a healthy and balanced lifestyle.

The WHO 5 a day initiative stems from extensive research showing that the vitamins, minerals, antioxidants and fibre found in five varying whole fruits and vegetables provides our body with the nutrients it needs for all our systems to function as efficiently as possible. The WHO states that eating a minimum of 400g (14oz) fruit and vegetables a day can reduce the risk of health issues such as heart disease, diabetes, high cholesterol, high blood pressure, stroke and selected types of cancer. You will see for yourself the list of nutrients provided by each of our recipes, which makes it clear how much we can help ourselves with what we eat.

As well as being delicious and colourful (and low in fat and calories), fruit and vegetables can boost our immune system, provide a fantastic source of energy, and help to ensure that we are fit and healthy in the long term.

5 a day and the four seasons

These days, when you go to the supermarket, you can pretty much buy whatever you want at any time of year. If a fruit or vegetable is out of season it will have been flown in from elsewhere around the world so that availability is continuous all year round.

When incorporating 5 a day into your lifestyle, it can be handy to know when different types of fruits and vegetables are in season. This is because when foods are in season, they are thriving, they taste better and there are more of them to buy and turn into delicious meals. You might notice that foods that are in season are often more affordable, giving you the perfect opportunity to buy in bulk and freeze them to enjoy during periods when they may be out of season. (By the way, frozen fruit and vegetables are great. They will have been freshly frozen soon after picking, retaining all their goodness. Indeed, the nutritional quality of frozen fruit and veg can often surpass the quality of fresh produce that has spent a fair amount of time travelling before it reaches your plate!)

Our seasonality chart opposite offers you a quick reference for when different fruits and vegetables are in season, so you know what to look out for.

SPRING

Broccoli, Cabbage, Cauliflower, Celeriac, Cucumber, Leeks, Onions, Peppers, Spring Onions

SUMMER

Asparagus, Aubergine, Beetroot, Cabbage, Carrots, Courgettes, Cucumber, Lettuce, Mangetout, Mushrooms, Onions, Peas, Peppers, Samphire, Spring Onions, Strawberries, Tomatoes

AUTUMN

Apples, Aubergine, Beetroot, Broccoli, Brussels Sprouts, Cabbage, Celeriac, Celery, Kale, Leeks, Lettuce, Onions, Parsnips, Peas, Peppers, Spring Onions, Squash, Sweetcorn, Tomatoes, Turnips

WINTER

Apples, Beetroot, Brussels Sprouts, Cabbage, Cauliflower, Celeriac, Celery, Kale, Leeks, Onions, Parsnips, Spring Onions, Turnips

Avoiding food waste: storing vegetables, fruit and herbs

The idea of this book is to help you eat your 5 a day and incorporate a wide variety of fruit and vegetables into your everyday life. We are well aware that, in buying the fruit, vegetables and herbs that you'll need for these recipes, you could find yourself with extra quantities of each, for which you have no immediate use. These extras need not go to waste if they are stored correctly. We have some suggestions on how to store them, so you don't end up with wilting leaves languishing at the back of the fridge.

Frozen

Frozen foods have suffered over the years from a degree of snobbery, with many people assuming that fresh must be best. However, frozen produce usually contains more goodness in the form of nutrients than its fresh counterpart, especially if the 'fresh' food has been on a long, protracted journey before it even reaches your local grocer or supermarket. Frozen fruit, herbs and vegetables are freshly picked and frozen straightaway, so all the goodness is retained without the chance for any deterioration to occur. The added benefit of frozen is, of course, that there is far less wastage because it lasts so much longer. In fact, we are convinced that in the coming years, we will see the freezer taking on greater importance in our kitchens than the fridge. With the UK currently wasting a jaw-dropping total of 4.5 million tonnes (5 million tons) of food annually, we think we should all 'hail the freezer' as soon as possible!

Fresh fruits

Keeping fruit in the fruit bowl is fine if you have a household that munches through the fruit on a daily basis. Even then, it's best to not wash it until you're ready to eat it, as that will help preserve it for a day or two longer. Unfortunately, fruits like apples, pears and bananas all release gas that helps to ripen their fellow fruits even more rapidly. Keeping apples, pears and soft fruits, like plums and apricots, in the fridge until you're ready to use them will help them last longer. If your fruit does become overripe, it doesn't need to go to waste. Brown, ripe bananas make delicious banana bread as well as excellent smoothies. Spare berries can be whizzed up into purées and freeze really well.

Fresh vegetables

Remove vegetable tops from carrots, parsnips, beetroots and turnips, as these suck moisture from the roots, making the vegetable dry out more quickly. If you buy your vegetables in a plastic bag from the supermarket, take them out of the bag as soon as possible and store them loose in the fridge. Storing root vegetables in the fridge in a covered bowl with a little water will prevent them from drying out. Meanwhile, onions should be kept in a cool, dark environment. If it's too warm, they will sprout; if it's too cold, they'll go damp and rot. Onions make up the base for many of our soups and stews, so dicing, blanching and freezing some is a good idea, as you'll always have some on hand when you're in a little bit of a pinch!

Fresh herbs

To keep herbs fresher for longer, dampen some kitchen paper, wrap it around the leaves and place in a food bag in the fridge. This should keep the herbs fresh for about a week. Alternatively, store herbs in mason jars in the fridge with a little water at the bottom to extend their life.

General advice

With all fruits and vegetables, wait to wash them until you're ready to eat or use them, and then only wash what you need. If you've opened a can of vegetables and have some left over, empty the remains into a covered bowl and store in the fridge, where they will last a couple of days. You can find out more about reducing food waste by heading over to @soupologie on Instagram to see more tips, tricks and recipes as part of our 'Food Waste Fridays' initiative.

light
soups

Pea & watercress soup

*Per serving 345 kcals | 18g fat | 1.4g saturates | 28.4g carbohydrates | 12.1g protein | 19.6g sugars
Vitamins A, C, E, K, B1 & B6, Folate, Potassium, Iron & Manganese*

This recipe is a great way to celebrate the distinctive peppery taste of watercress, complemented by the lovely sweet notes of peas and apples. Plant-powered Soupologistas take note: vegans and vegetarians can be prone to lacking in vitamin K, but watercress is packed with it. Vitamin K is vital for healthy blood and bones, and can help protect against osteoporosis.

1. Heat the oil in a medium saucepan over a low heat. Add the onions and cook for 3–4 minutes, stirring regularly. Add the garlic and parsley and season with salt and pepper. Cook for a further 5 minutes until the onions have turned translucent and are starting to caramelize.

2. Pour in the vegetable stock. Now you can add in the peas, apples, watercress and spinach. Increase the heat and bring to the boil, then reduce to a simmer for 5–7 minutes.

3. Take off the heat and blend the soup with a hand blender or in a food processor until completely smooth. Divide between two bowls and serve, garnished with the reserved apple and watercress.

SERVES 2

2 tablespoons vegetable oil
2 medium onions (160g/5¾oz), chopped
2 garlic cloves, finely chopped
1 teaspoon dried parsley
700ml (1¼ pints) vegetable stock (page 114)
160g (5¾oz) peas, fresh or frozen
2 apples (about 160g/5¾oz), peeled, cored and chopped, reserving a handful to garnish
160g (5¾oz) watercress, plus extra to garnish
160g (5¾oz) spinach, fresh or frozen
salt and freshly ground black pepper, to taste

Turmeric broth

Per serving 259 kcals | 7.6g fat | 0.7g saturates | 33.2g carbohydrates | 9.2g protein | 11.5g sugars
Vitamins A & C, Folate & Potassium

The turmeric base of this broth is delicious and earthy with a zesty freshness that comes from the gut-friendly garlic and ginger. Here, we've rounded it out with chickpeas, kale, noodles and fresh coriander, but you can customize with other vegetables. Try it with cauliflower, courgette, black beans and sweet potato.

1. Heat the oil in a large saucepan over a low heat. Add the onion, ginger, garlic, carrots and celery. Stir in the turmeric and ground coriander. Cook for 5 minutes, stirring occasionally, until the vegetables start to soften and the onion turns translucent.

2. Now, you can mix in the chickpeas, kale or spinach and cayenne pepper (if using). Sprinkle over salt and pepper to taste. Cook for 1 minute more, then pour in the stock. Add the noodles immediately and bring the soup to the boil. Reduce the heat to a simmer for about 5 minutes or until the noodles are cooked.

3. Take off the heat, squeeze over the lime juice and serve, topped with fresh coriander. Enjoy!

SERVES 2

1 tablespoon vegetable oil

2 medium onions (160g/5¾oz), diced

1–2 tablespoons freshly grated ginger

1 garlic clove, minced

2 medium carrots (160g/5¾oz), peeled and diced

3 large celery sticks (160g/5¾oz), trimmed and finely sliced

1 teaspoon ground turmeric

1 teaspoon ground coriander

160g (5¾oz) canned chickpeas

160g (5¾oz) kale or spinach

pinch of cayenne pepper (optional)

800ml (1½ pints) vegetable stock (page 114)

80g (2¾oz) rice noodles

juice of ½ lime

handful of fresh coriander, chopped

salt and freshly ground black pepper, to taste

Nettle, spinach & wheatgrass soup

Per serving 210 kcals | 9.9g fat | 1g saturates | 16.5g carbohydrates | 9.3g protein | 10g sugars
Vitamins A, C & B6, Folate, Potassium, Calcium, Iron & Manganese

Nettle and wheatgrass are exceptionally interesting ingredients to use in cooking. Their taste is earthy and lightly spiced, and if you buy good-quality powders, they are so full of vitamins, iron and goodness that they practically do press-ups in front of your eyes. This soup is packed with iron-rich spinach and kale; beta-carotene is provided by the carrots, and the samphire provides all the salt you need without having to add any extra.

1. Heat the oil in a large saucepan over a low–medium heat. Add the leek, garlic, carrots, parsley, thyme, nutmeg, cinnamon and black pepper. Cook for 5–7 minutes, stirring occasionally, until the vegetables have started to soften and the leeks have turned translucent.

2. Now you can add the samphire, nettle powder and wheatgrass powder. Give everything a good stir, then pour in the vegetable stock. Partially cover the pan with a lid and bring to the boil for about 30 seconds, then reduce to a simmer.

3. Remove the lid and add the spinach and kale to the saucepan. You might want to add them in stages, using a wooden spoon to push them down into the liquid until they begin to wilt and there is space to add the rest. Now partially cover the pan again and bring back up to a simmer for 5 minutes.

4. Blend the soup with a hand blender or in a food processor until completely smooth (see Tip).

5. Serve and enjoy the burst of green!

SERVES 2

1 tablespoon vegetable oil
1 medium leek (160g/5¾oz), trimmed and roughly chopped
1 garlic clove, roughly chopped
2 medium carrots, (160g/5¾oz), peeled and chopped
1 teaspoon dried parsley
½ teaspoon dried thyme
¼ teaspoon ground nutmeg
pinch of cinnamon
¼ teaspoon freshly ground black pepper
160g (5¾oz) samphire
1 teaspoon nettle powder
1 teaspoon wheatgrass powder
500ml (18fl oz) vegetable stock (page 114)
160g (5¾oz) spinach
160g (5¾oz) kale
handful of chives, chopped, to serve

TIP: *We recommend that you blend this soup really well. When you think you have blended it enough, blend it one more time! The tough stalks from the kale can take a while to break down into a smooth soup.*

Leek & sauerkraut soup

Per serving 267 kcals | 9.1g fat | 0.9g saturates | 28.8g carbohydrates | 10.5g protein | 17.9g sugars
Vitamins C, B1 & B6, Folate & Potassium

Being a rare source of vitamin K2, plant-powered people should turn to sauerkraut for healthy cardiovascular, blood and bone function. It's also packed with probiotics, which are beneficial for our gut flora and overall digestive health. In this recipe, we've opted to use agave nectar as a sweetener since it's low on the glycaemic index (GI), making it a healthy sugar (and vegan!) alternative to honey. The mild flavour of the butter beans lessens the vinegary kick of the sauerkraut, and they're a great source of protein.

1. Heat the oil in a medium saucepan over a medium heat. Add the leek, cauliflower, turnips, white cabbage and nutmeg. Cook, stirring regularly, for 5–10 minutes, until the vegetables begin to soften and the leek starts to turn translucent.

2. Now add the mustard powder (if using), sweet paprika and bay leaf. Season with salt and pepper. Stir briefly, then pour in the vegetable stock. Increase the heat and bring the soup to a boil for 30 seconds, then reduce the heat to a simmer. Cover the pan with a lid and simmer for 2 minutes.

3. Add the butter beans, sauerkraut and agave nectar (if using) to the soup. Cover once again and return to a simmer for a further 3 minutes.

4. Take the soup off the heat. Find and remove the bay leaf, then blend the soup with a hand blender or in a food processor until smooth. Taste for seasoning, then serve and enjoy!

SERVES 2

1 tablespoon vegetable oil
1 medium leek (160g/5¾oz), trimmed and chopped
160g (5¾oz) cauliflower florets
2 turnips (160g/5¾oz), peeled and chopped
140g (5oz) white cabbage, roughly chopped
¼ teaspoon ground nutmeg
¼ teaspoon mustard powder (optional)
a couple of pinches of sweet paprika
1 bay leaf
500ml (18fl oz) vegetable stock (page 114)
160g (5¾oz) butter beans
20g (¾oz) sauerkraut
1 tablespoon agave nectar (optional)
salt and freshly ground black pepper, to taste

TIP: *If you're feeling adventurous, why not turn to purple cabbage instead of white? A pop of purple rarely features in our diets and brightly coloured soup is sure to make for interesting dinner party conversation!*

Lentil, lemon & spinach soup

Per serving 482 kcals | 25g fat | 4.6g saturates | 38.7g carbohydrates | 19.2g protein | 8.6g sugars
Vitamins A, C, B1 & B6, Folate, Potassium, Phosphorus, Iron, Copper & Manganese

Let's start with a little-known fact: all lentil varieties are made up of over 25 per cent protein. They are also a great source of iron and we've combined them in this soup with spinach, making this a super iron-rich dish! Iron is essential for healthy red blood cells and oxygen transportation around the body, so this is a wonderfully comforting soup to fall back on when you're feeling a bit fatigued and worn out. Vitamin C-rich foods, like lemon, help our body to absorb iron. Serve this soup with avocado on toast to meet your full 5 a day.

1. Heat the oil in a medium saucepan over a low heat. Add the onion, celery, garlic and turmeric. Season with salt and pepper. Cook for 5–10 minutes, stirring occasionally, until the vegetables are soft and the onions are just beginning to turn translucent.

2. Add the lentils to the saucepan and stir them thoroughly into the onion mixture. Pour in the stock, increase the heat and bring to a boil with the saucepan partially covered with a lid. Reduce the heat and let the soup simmer, covered, for a further 15 minutes. Stir regularly and check to see if the lentils are soft and beginning to break apart. If not, keep the soup simmering with the lid on for 5 more minutes. Squeeze the lemon juice into the soup and add the spinach, stirring over a low heat until the spinach has wilted.

3. Remove the soup from the heat and blend with a hand blender or in a food processor until you have reached the desired consistency. Stir in a dollop of vegan yogurt and serve with avocado on toast on the side.

SERVES 2

2 tablespoons olive oil
2 medium onions (160g/5¾oz), chopped
3 celery sticks (160g/5¾oz), trimmed and chopped
1 garlic clove, chopped
1 teaspoon ground turmeric
160g (5¾oz) dried green lentils
750ml (1⅓ pints) vegetable stock (page 114)
juice of 1 lemon
160g (5¾oz) spinach, fresh or frozen
salt and freshly ground black pepper

To serve
a few dollops of vegan yogurt (optional)
1 avocado (160g/5¾oz), sliced or mashed
toast (we suggest rye bread)

TIP: *This soup thickens over time, so you can eat a second portion later as a stew or add more hot water to the soup to thin it out.*

Earthy beetroot soup

*Per serving 357 kcals | 13g fat | 1.2g saturates | 48.7g carbohydrates | 6g protein | 40.6g sugars
Vitamins A, C & B6, Folate, Potassium & Manganese*

This comforting soup is just perfect for the winter months. Beetroot is a great source of fibre and also contains high amounts of folate, which is important for the maintenance of our cells and tissues. The pomegranate juice is packed full of antioxidants, which protect our cells from damage by removing harmful free radicals. They're also linked with reducing inflammation.

1. Heat the oil in a medium saucepan over a medium heat and add the onions, carrots and parsnips. Cook for 3–4 minutes, then sprinkle over the coriander and nutmeg, and season with salt and pepper.

2. Cook for a further 5 minutes or until the vegetables have started to soften, then add the beetroot. Stir and cook for 2–3 minutes more, then pour in the pomegranate juice and vegetable stock.

3. Increase the heat and bring the soup to the boil for 1 minute, then reduce to a simmer for a further 5 minutes. Take off the heat and blend the soup with a hand blender or in a food processor until silky smooth. Taste for seasoning, then divide between two bowls and serve topped with a sprinkling of pomegranate seeds if using. Enjoy!

SERVES 2

1½ tablespoons vegetable oil
2 medium onions (160g/5¾oz), chopped
2 medium carrots (160g/5¾oz), peeled and chopped
2 medium parsnips (160g/5¾oz), peeled and chopped
½ teaspoon ground coriander
¼ teaspoon ground nutmeg
200g (7oz) ready-cooked beetroot, cubed
300ml (½ pint) unsweetened pomegranate juice
150ml (¼ pint) vegetable stock (page 114)
salt and freshly ground black pepper, to taste
handful of pomegranate seeds, to serve (optional)

Lettuce, cucumber & pea soup

Per serving 306 kcals | 17g fat | 1.2g saturates | 22.2g carbohydrates | 10g protein | 16g sugars
Vitamins A, C, & B1, Folate, Potassium & Manganese

This soup evokes a lovely late spring day. It's perfect for when the seasons are changing, along with our food choices. The mint boosts the whole dish with a cool, crisp sensation. Lettuce is one of the most wasted vegetables in many households (doesn't it always seem to wilt quickly even when kept in the fridge?), so this recipe will handily use up any lettuce leaves that would otherwise be discarded. To elevate it to 6 a day, you could pair it with the kale crisps featured on page 120.

1. Heat the oil in a large saucepan over a low heat. Add the onions and cook for 5–7 minutes or until soft and lightly golden.

2. Add the cucumber, peas and spinach. Stir well and cook for 3–4 minutes, or for a bit longer if you are using frozen spinach, as you will want the spinach to have largely thawed before moving on to the next stage.

3. Pour in the vegetable stock, increase the heat and bring the soup to the boil for 1 minute. Reduce the heat and stir in the lettuce and mint. Simmer for a further 5 minutes, partially covered with a lid.

4. Take the soup off the heat and blend with a hand blender or in a food processor until smooth. Serve and enjoy topped with chopped mint leaves! It's also delicious served cold for a refreshing boost on a warm day.

SERVES 2

2 tablespoons vegetable oil
2 medium onions (160g/5¾oz), chopped
160g (5¾oz) cucumber
160g (5¾oz) peas, fresh or frozen
160g (5¾oz) spinach, fresh or frozen
700ml (1¼ pints) vegetable stock (page 114)
160g (5¾oz) lettuce, such as romaine or iceberg, chopped
small handful of freshly chopped mint, plus extra to serve
salt and freshly ground black pepper, to taste

Celeriac & grape soup

Per serving 259 kcals | 7.6g fat | 0.7g saturates | 33.2g carbohydrates | 9.2g protein | 11.5g sugars
Vitamins A & C, Folate & Potassium

Pairing grapes with celeriac feels quite gastronomic and fancy, but this is a great dish to introduce younger foodies to the world of culinary delights. It might seem bonkers to have grapes in a soup, but their sweet, slightly tart taste perfectly complements the peppery watercress and nutty celeriac.

1. Heat the oil in a medium-sized saucepan over a medium heat and add the onions. Cook for 3–4 minutes until they begin to caramelize. Add the green peppers and celeriac and cook for a further 3–4 minutes.

2. Stir in the watercress, grapes, spinach and parsley, and season with salt and pepper.

3. Pour in the vegetable stock. Increase the heat and bring the soup to the boil, then reduce the heat and simmer for 5–10 minutes with the lid partially on.

4. Take the soup off the heat and blend with a hand blender or in a food processor until completely smooth.

5. Taste for seasoning, serve topped with a couple of halved grapes and enjoy!

SERVES 2

1 tablespoon vegetable oil
2 medium onions (160g/5¾oz), chopped
2 green peppers (160g/5¾oz), deseeded and chopped
160g (5¾oz) celeriac, peeled and chopped
160g (5¾oz) watercress
160g (5¾oz) green grapes, halved, plus extra to garnish
160g (5¾oz) spinach, fresh or frozen
handful of freshly chopped parsley
400ml (14fl oz) vegetable stock (page 114)
salt and freshly ground black pepper, to taste

TIP: *If you can eat nuts, this delectable soup is great with some chopped roasted hazelnuts scattered on top to serve.*

Artichoke, spinach & red pepper soup

*Per serving 333 kcals | 1.3g fat | 1.3g saturates | 31.3g carbohydrates | 11.6g protein | 11g sugars
Vitamins A & C, Folate, Potassium & Manganese*

This soup is a cheeky twist on a classic dip – red pepper and artichoke hummus! Chickpeas are a great source of plant-based protein. They contain all the essential amino acids our bodies need except for methionine (which you can get from whole grains). Artichokes, on the other hand, have many antioxidant properties and are beneficial for our blood sugar and cholesterol levels.

1. Heat the oil in a medium-sized saucepan over a low heat. Add the onions and garlic. Cook on a low heat for 2–3 minutes until slightly softened but not brown. Now add the red peppers and coriander, and season with salt and pepper.

2. Cook for a further 2–3 minutes until the onion turns translucent and the peppers are soft. Now add the artichokes, spinach and chickpeas. Stir regularly for a few minutes until the spinach is wilted. This might take a bit longer if using frozen spinach.

3. Now squeeze the lemon juice into the saucepan and pour over the vegetable stock.

4. Increase the heat and bring the soup to the boil, then reduce to a simmer for 5 minutes with the saucepan partially covered by the lid.

5. Remove from the heat and blend with a hand blender or in a food processor until completely smooth. Divide between two bowls and serve with some extra chickpeas scattered on top for a chunkier texture.

SERVES 2

2 tablespoons vegetable oil
2 medium onions (160g/5¾oz), chopped
4 garlic cloves, finely chopped
2 red peppers (160g/5¾oz), deseeded and chopped
handful of freshly chopped coriander
160g (5¾oz) jarred chargrilled artichokes
160g (5¾oz) spinach, fresh or frozen
160g (5¾oz) canned chickpeas, drained, plus extra to serve
juice of ½ lemon
500ml (18fl oz) vegetable stock (page 114)
salt and freshly ground black pepper, to taste

Cold courgette & avocado soup

Per serving 351 kcals | 24g fat | 4.9g saturates | 20.2g carbohydrates | 8.5g protein | 14.9g sugars
Vitamins A, B1, B6 & C, Folate & Potassium

We always look forward to making cold soups as summer approaches; they are a great way to stay hydrated during the blistering heat. We've gone for the fresh, crisp taste of mint and coriander here, but feel free to be creative and experiment with using different herbs!

1. Heat the oil in a medium saucepan over a low heat. Add the onion, garlic, courgette and cauliflower. Cook, stirring regularly, for 5 minutes until the vegetables begin to soften.

2. Season with salt and pepper and stir to combine. Add the tomato purée and mix well to spread it evenly among the vegetables. Pour in the vegetable stock, increase the heat and bring the soup to a boil. Cover the saucepan with a lid and reduce the heat to a simmer. Simmer for 5 minutes.

3. Remove the soup from the heat and blend with a hand blender or in a food processor until smooth. Allow the soup to cool slightly in the saucepan, then transfer it to a large bowl and place in the refrigerator for at least 3 hours or until cold.

4. Remove the soup from the refrigerator and add the avocado, mint, coriander, lime juice, chilli and balsamic vinegar (if using).

5. Blend again until smooth, then taste for seasoning. Serve cold topped with fresh herbs and chilli (if using) and enjoy!

SERVES 2

1 tablespoon olive oil

2 medium onions (160g/5¾oz), chopped

1 garlic clove, chopped

1 large courgette (160g/5¾oz), trimmed and sliced into rounds

160g (5¾oz) cauliflower florets

2 tablespoons double-concentrated tomato purée

500ml (18fl oz) vegetable stock (page 114)

1 large Hass avocado (160g/5¾oz), peeled, pitted and chopped

1 tablespoon fresh mint leaves, plus extra to serve

1 tablespoon fresh coriander leaves, plus extra to serve

juice of ½ lime

¼ red chilli, deseeded, plus extra to serve (optional)

2 teaspoons balsamic vinegar (optional)

salt and freshly ground black pepper, to taste

Cucumber & avocado gazpacho

Per serving 417 kcals | 32g fat | 5.6g saturates | 15.6g carbohydrates | 9.6g protein | 10.1g sugars
Vitamins B1, B6 & C, Folate, Potassium, Copper & Manganese

This cold soup is lovely in the summer. The sweetness of the peas contrasts with the heat of the chilli. If you prefer a spicier soup, you can add more chilli; for a milder, more refreshing flavour, you can swap the chilli for some cool mint. We've included two kinds of vinegar, but the fruity-tart taste of balsamic vinegar is not overpowering at all. Keeping the skin on the cucumber ensures you get the maximum fibre and nutrients available. It also helps to provide a luscious green colour during the blend.

1. Place all the ingredients in a food processor and blend until completely smooth. Serve and enjoy!

SERVES 2

½ cucumber (160g/5¾oz), chopped
160g (5¾oz) peas, fresh or defrosted
2 red peppers (160g/5¾oz), deseeded and chopped
1 avocado (160g/5¾oz), peeled, pitted and roughly chopped
160g (5¾oz) fresh spinach
2 tablespoons olive oil
1 tablespoon apple cider vinegar
2 teaspoons balsamic vinegar
1 garlic clove, chopped
¼–½ teaspoon green chilli, deseeded and chopped
300ml (½ pint) water
salt and freshly ground black pepper, to taste

Watermelon & chilli gazpacho

Per serving 177 kcals | 7.2g fat | 1.1g saturates | 17.7g carbohydrates | 6.4g protein | 16.5g sugars
Vitamins B6 & C, Folate & Potassium

This gazpacho makes a divine addition to a summery meal. It's always satisfying to see even the most determined of 'I only eat soup hot' diehards enjoying every last drop! Watermelons are 92 per cent water, meaning they will quench your thirst and leave you feeling fuller for longer. Cucumbers go one better, with a water content of 95 per cent. We use aromatic basil to season this gazpacho, and it works well with the tomatoes and red peppers, but do experiment with other herbs if you wish.

1. Place the red onion in a small bowl and pour over the red wine vinegar. Set aside for 10 minutes.

2. Add all the other ingredients to a blender and blend until smooth. Pour in the red onion and vinegar mixture and blend again until fully combined. Taste for seasoning. Serve and enjoy on a sunny day with a sprinkling of basil!

SERVES 1

¼ red onion, chopped
½ tablespoon red wine vinegar
80g (2¾oz) watermelon chunks
80g (2¾oz) cucumber, skin on
80g (2¾oz) tomatoes
80g (2¾oz) cauliflower florets
80g (2¾oz) red pepper, deseeded
1 teaspoon extra virgin olive oil
¼ –½ small green chilli, deseeded
handful of basil, plus extra to serve
salt and freshly ground black pepper, to taste

comfort soups

Sweet potato, apple & maple soup

Per serving 323 kcals | 8.8g fat | 1.4g saturates | 51.4g carbohydrates | 4.4g protein | 32.3g sugars
Vitamins B & C, Potassium & Manganese

The dominant flavours in this soup are the rich and creamy sweet potato and butternut squash, coupled with the caramel-like goodness that is maple syrup. The apples add a fresh and tart piquancy while also providing one serving of your 5 a day. The Brussels sprouts crisps make an unusual, but fabulous, accompaniment and have even proven popular with family, friends and children with a historic dislike for sprouts. Plus, unlike regular crisps, these count as one of your 5 a day!

1. Heat the oil in a large saucepan over a low heat. Add the onions, butternut squash, sweet potatoes, garlic, thyme, sage and nutmeg. Season with the salt and pepper.

2. Cook, stirring regularly, for about 10 minutes, until the vegetables have started to soften and the onion has turned translucent. Keep an eye on the heat and make sure the garlic does not begin to burn.

3. Pour in the vegetable stock. Increase the heat and bring the soup to a boil for 30 seconds. Reduce the heat and simmer for 2 minutes.

4. Stir the apples into the soup and drizzle in the maple syrup into the saucepan. Simmer for another 3 minutes, then take off the heat.

5. Blend the soup with a hand blender or in a food processor until super smooth. Top with the Brussels sprouts crisps and a sprinkling of pumpkin seeds. Serve and enjoy!

SERVES 4

2 tablespoons olive oil
4 medium onions (320g/11½oz), chopped
1 butternut squash (320g/11½oz), peeled, deseeded and cubed
2 large sweet potatoes (320g/11½oz), peeled and chopped
2 garlic cloves, chopped
1 teaspoon dried thyme
1 teaspoon dried sage
½ teaspoon ground nutmeg
1 litre (1¾ pints) vegetable stock (page 114)
3 eating apples (320g/11½oz), such as Pink Lady or Red Delicious, peeled, cored and chopped
3 tablespoons maple syrup
salt and freshly ground black pepper, to taste

To serve
Brussels sprouts crisps (page 118)
handful of pumpkin seeds

Sweetcorn chowder with samphire

Per serving 266 kcals | 9.2g fat | 0.9g saturates | 33g carbohydrates | 8.6g protein | 20.1g sugars
Vitamins A, C, B1, B6 & B12, Iron, Folate & Potassium

Vegans rejoice! This soup has all the flavours of the sea with none of the fish. Available near the fish counter at the supermarket, samphire is a vibrant green sea vegetable with a lovely salty flavour (so no need to add any extra salt to this recipe when seasoning). Its flavour is perfectly balanced out by the sweetcorn, carrots and cauliflower. Sweetcorn is rich in vitamins A, B6 and C, plus it's a complex carbohydrate, which means it releases energy slowly over time.

1. Heat the oil in a large saucepan and add the onions, garlic and carrots. Cook over a low heat for 5 minutes, stirring occasionally, or until the onions turn translucent and are starting to caramelize.

2. Add the cauliflower florets to the saucepan, along with the samphire and chives. Season with black pepper. Cook for 2–3 minutes, stirring regularly to avoid any vegetables burning. Pour in the vegetable stock.

3. Increase the heat and bring the soup to a boil, then reduce to a simmer. Add the sweetcorn. If you would like a chunkier finish to your soup, reserve 100g (3½oz) of the sweetcorn to add later. Bring the soup back up to a simmer.

4. Cook for a further 5 minutes, then take off the heat. Blend with a hand blender or in a food processor until you get a silky-smooth soup – the smoother the better with this recipe. If you have set aside some of the sweetcorn, stir it through now. Scatter over some samphire and enjoy!

SERVES 2

1 tablespoon vegetable oil
2 medium onions (160g/5¾oz), chopped
1 garlic clove, chopped
2 medium carrots (160g/5¾oz), peeled and chopped
160g (5¾oz) cauliflower florets
160g (5¾oz) samphire, plus extra to garnish
good handful of chopped chives, plus extra to serve
600ml (20fl oz) vegetable stock (page 114)
320g (11½oz) sweetcorn, tinned or frozen
cracked black pepper, to taste

Celeriac, apple & cider soup

Per serving 219 kcals | 10g fat | 1.2g saturates | 19.1g carbohydrates | 6.9g protein | 16g sugars
Vitamins B1, B6 & C, Folate & Potassium

Celeriac provides one portion of your 5 a day and might seem like an awkward veg to work with at first, but it's extremely versatile. We've sneaked in a leek and cauliflower florets, which not only contribute to the silky texture when blended, but it's also an easy way to incorporate veggies into the diets of fussy eaters.

1. Peel and roughly chop the leek, celeriac and garlic. Heat the vegetable oil in a medium saucepan. Add in the leeks, celeriac, cauliflower, garlic, nutmeg and mustard powder. Season with salt and pepper.

2. Turn the heat down to medium-low and stir the vegetables regularly to prevent the leeks from burning. When the vegetables have softened slightly and the leeks have turned translucent, about 5 minutes, pour in the vegetable stock.

3. Turn the heat up and bring the soup to a boil. Keep it boiling for 30 seconds then turn it down to a simmer for 3 minutes.

4. Peel, core and cube the Bramley apple. Add the apples and the cider to the soup. Simmer for a further 2 minutes, keeping the lid partially on – this is to retain as much water as possible in the soup.

5. Remove from the heat and blend until completely smooth. Taste for seasoning and smoothness. Blend again for an extra silky soup.

6. Top the soup with kale crisps and serve.

SERVES 2

1 tablespoon vegetable oil
1 medium leek (160g/5¾oz), trimmed and roughly chopped
160g (5¾oz) celeriac, peeled and roughly chopped
160g (5¾oz) cauliflower florets
1 garlic clove, roughly chopped
½ teaspoon ground nutmeg
¼ teaspoon mustard powder (optional)
500ml (18fl oz) vegetable stock
2 Bramley apples (160g/5¾oz), peeled, cored and cubed
1½ tablespoons apple cider
salt and freshly ground black pepper

To serve
kale crisps (page 120)

Chunky vegetable soup

*Per serving 234 kcals | 7.7g fat | 0.6g saturates | 30.4g carbohydrates | 6.4g protein | 16.6g sugars
Vitamins C, B1 & B6, Folate & Potassium*

One of the best things about this staple soup is that you can accessorize it and make it your own. This is just a basic guide based around some excellent root vegetables. It's a great opportunity to use up any leftover veggies, as you can easily substitute vegetables. We've used white potatoes here as we like the substantial, starchy texture that they provide, but they won't count towards your 5 a day (see page 9).

1. Heat the oil in a large saucepan over a medium heat. Reduce the heat to low and add the onions, garlic and carrots. Cook for about 5 minutes, stirring occasionally, or until just starting to soften.

2. Add the potatoes, turnips and courgettes. Cook for a further 5 minutes, stirring to prevent the potatoes from sticking to the bottom of the pan.

3. Stir in the parsley and turmeric, and season with salt and pepper. Pour in the canned tomatoes. Increase the heat and cook for 1 minute, stirring frequently, before tipping in the vegetable stock.

4. Bring the soup to a boil for 1 minute, then reduce the heat to a low simmer for a further 15 minutes. Although this is a chunky soup, you don't want the liquid to become too thick or too thin: aim for a syrupy texture.

5. When the soup has reached the desired texture, remove it from the heat, taste for seasoning and serve. Top with a sprinkle of fresh parsley and a side of crusty bread for a filling and wholesome dinner!

SERVES 4

2 tablespoons vegetable oil

4 medium onions (320g/11½oz), diced

3 garlic cloves, diced

4 medium carrots (320g/11½oz), peeled and cut into rounds

2 medium white potatoes (320g/11½oz), cubed

4 turnips (320g/11½oz), peeled and chopped

2 courgettes (320g/11½oz), chopped

large handful of freshly chopped flat-leaf parsley, plus extra to serve

1 teaspoon ground turmeric

1 x 400g (14oz) can chopped tomatoes

800ml (1½ pints) vegetable stock (page 114)

salt and freshly ground black pepper, to taste

Mushroom, leek & asparagus soup

Per serving 307 kcals | 18g fat | 2.6g saturates | 19.1g carbohydrates | 6.9g protein | 16g sugars
Vitamins A, C, B1 & B6, Folate, Potassium, Phosphorus, Iron, Copper & Magnesium

Whatever type of mushroom you adore you'll be pleased to know that they contain protein, fibre and B vitamins. They are also a source of selenium, which is integral to a healthy immune system. If there's even a tiny bit of sunshine in autumn, we like to keep them in the sunlight for 30 minutes prior to cooking for that extra boost of vitamin D, which the mushrooms will happily absorb.

1. Heat the oil in a medium-sized saucepan over a low heat and add the leeks. Cook for 3–4 minutes until soft and slightly translucent.

2. Add the garlic and thyme and cook for another minute, then stir in the mushrooms, asparagus, spinach and peas. Cook, stirring regularly, for a further 5–10 minutes or until the vegetables have softened.

3. Pour in the vegetable stock, increase the heat and bring the soup to the boil for 1 minute. Reduce to a simmer for 5 minutes, then take off the heat and blend with a hand blender or in a food processor until smooth. Divide between two bowls and serve.

SERVES 2

2 tablespoons olive oil
1 medium leek (160g/5¾oz), chopped
2 garlic cloves, chopped
1 teaspoon dried thyme
160g (5¾oz) chestnut mushrooms, chopped
160g (5¾oz) asparagus (see Tip), ends trimmed and chopped
160g (5¾oz) spinach, fresh or frozen
160g (5¾oz) peas, fresh or frozen
500ml (18floz) vegetable stock (page 114)
salt and freshly ground black pepper, to taste

TIP: *You can experiment with the type of asparagus you use in this soup. White asparagus is usually chunkier, with a slightly sweeter taste compared to the grassy flavour of green asparagus. If you're feeling particularly adventurous, purple asparagus is much milder, but even sweeter!*

Roasted squash & apple soup

Per serving 257 kcals | 9.6g fat | 0.7g saturates | 33.4g carbohydrates | 4.1g protein | 26.4g sugars
Vitamins A & C, Potassium

Nothing is more autumnal than a deliciously ripe butternut squash. Roasting the squash until the edges are ever so slightly crisp and burnt adds a warming depth of flavour and toastiness to this soup. Choose the apple according to the level of sweetness you prefer.

1. Preheat the oven to 240°C/220°C fan/475°F/gas mark 9 and line a baking sheet with baking paper.

2. Arrange the chopped butternut squash and carrots on the baking tray in one even layer. Drizzle over 1 tablespoon of the oil and scatter over the nutmeg, along with some salt and pepper. Roast for 15–20 minutes, or until the vegetables have started to crisp up.

3. Meanwhile, heat the remaining oil in a large saucepan over a low heat. Add the onions, garlic and ginger. Cook for 5 minutes, stirring occasionally, until the onions turn translucent and are beginning to caramelize. Season with salt and pepper.

4. Pour in the vegetable stock, increase the heat and bring to the boil for 30 seconds. Partially cover the saucepan with a lid and reduce the heat to a simmer and add the apple pieces. Simmer for a further 2 minutes.

5. Carefully add the roasted vegetables to the saucepan, partially cover with the lid once more and continue to simmer for a further 3 minutes. Take off the heat and blend with a hand blender or in a food processor until completely smooth.

6. Top with sweet potato chips, serve and enjoy!

SERVES 4

½ butternut squash
   (320g/11½oz), or squash
   of your choice, peeled,
   deseeded and cut into
   2.5-cm (1-inch) cubes
4 medium carrots
   (320g/11½oz), peeled and
   chopped into rounds
2 tablespoons vegetable oil
½ teaspoon nutmeg
4 medium onions
   (320g/11½oz), chopped
2 garlic cloves, chopped
1–2 tablespoons grated fresh
   ginger
800ml (1½ pints) vegetable
   stock (page 114)
4 eating apples (320g/11½oz),
   such as Pink Lady or Golden
   Delicious, peeled, cored and
   sliced
salt and freshly ground black
   pepper, to taste

To serve
sweet potato chips (page
   121 – we've sliced these
   widthways and reduced the
   baking time, keeping an eye
   on them so they don't burn)

Parsnip, pear & cranberry soup

Per serving 353 kcals | 10g fat | 0.8g saturates | 54.7g carbohydrates | 4.2g protein | 40.8g sugars
Vitamins B1 & C, Folate & Potassium

This is a perfect soup for the festive season, with creamy nuttiness from the parsnips, sweetness from the pears and bittersweet notes from the dried cranberries. It just oozes seasonal cheer. Parsnips are a great source of vitamin C, while pears contain lots of dietary fibre. Where possible, I would recommend buying unsweetened dried cranberries, as any dried fruit can add a significant amount of sugar to your diet.

1. Heat the oil in a large saucepan over a low heat. Add the onions, parsnips, celery and ground cardamom. Cook for 5 minutes, stirring occasionally, until the onions have turned translucent and are starting to caramelize. Season with salt and pepper and give the vegetables another stir.

2. Pour in the vegetable stock and bring the soup to the boil for 30 seconds. Now you can drop in the pears. Reduce the heat and simmer for a further 5 minutes, partially covered with a lid. Remove from the heat.

3. If you prefer, you can leave some or all of the cranberries whole and use them as a topping. In which case, blend the soup until smooth.

4. Alternatively, if you prefer to mix the cranberries into the soup, blend the soup first as it is, then drop in the cranberries and blend again briefly. (Don't blend too much after adding them, or the whole soup will turn bright pink – unless pink is the colour you're after!)

5. Serve with the reserved cranberries (if reserved) and enjoy!

SERVES 4

2 tablespoons vegetable oil

4 medium onions (320g/11½oz), chopped

4 medium parsnips (320g/11½oz), peeled and chopped

6 celery sticks (320g/11½oz), trimmed and sliced

½ teaspoon ground cardamom

800ml (1½ pints) vegetable stock (page 114)

4 pears (320g/11½oz), peeled, cored and diced

120g (4¼oz) dried cranberries

salt and freshly ground black pepper, to taste

TIP: *Add 1–2 tablespoons brandy to this soup just before serving for an extra Christmassy twist!*

Maple-balsamic glazed Brussels sprouts & sweet potato soup

Per serving *219 kcals | 10g fat | 1.2g saturates | 19.1g carbohydrates | 6.9g protein | 16g sugars*
Vitamins B, B6 & C, Folate & Potassium

This is our 5 a day variation of an all-American Thanksgiving. Sweet potatoes are rich in fibre and beta-carotene, which converts into vitamin A in the body. Brussels sprouts are a member of the Brassicaceae family and are rich in vitamin C.

1. Preheat oven to 240°C/220°C fan/475°F/gas mark 9 and line a baking sheet with tin foil.

2. In a large bowl, mix together the sweet potato, Brussels sprouts and carrots. Drizzle over 1 tablespoon of the vegetable oil, along with the balsamic vinegar, maple syrup, paprika and chilli flakes (if using). Season with salt and pepper. Toss together until fully coated in the glaze. Transfer to the prepared baking sheet in an even layer.

3. Roast for 20–25 minutes or until the vegetables start to turn golden brown, keeping an eye on their progress.

4. Heat the remaining vegetable oil in a large saucepan over a low heat. Pour in the onion, shallot and garlic and cook gently for about 10 minutes, stirring occasionally, until the onion has turned translucent and is just starting to caramelize.

5. Pour in the vegetable stock. Increase the heat and bring to the boil, then to a simmer for 2 minutes with the lid on. Now tip in the roasted vegetables and keep simmering, partially covered, for a further 2 minutes. Take off the heat and blend with a hand blender or in a food processor. When silky smooth, taste for seasoning and scatter over the parsnip crisps before serving.

SERVES 2

1 medium sweet potato (160g/5¾oz), peeled and roughly chopped
160g (5¾oz) Brussels sprouts, trimmed and halved
2 medium carrots (160g/5¾oz), peeled and roughly chopped
2 tablespoons vegetable oil
2 tablespoons balsamic vinegar or glaze
2 tablespoons maple syrup
¼ teaspoon sweet smoked paprika
pinch of chilli flakes (optional)
1 medium onion (80g/2¾oz), chopped
1 large shallot (80g/2¾oz), chopped
2 garlic cloves, chopped
750ml (1⅓ pints) vegetable stock (page 114)
salt and freshly ground black pepper, to taste

To serve
parsnip crisps (page 124)

Lentil dhal soup

Per serving 378 kcals | 12g fat | 1g saturates | 43.4g carbohydrates | 18.3g protein | 13.1g sugars Vitamins A, C, B1 & B6, Folate, Potassium, Iron & Copper

Dhal, daal, dail, dahl, dal! However you spell it, the name comes from the Sanskrit word meaning 'to split' – think split peas! Lentils are so versatile, rich in protein and easy-peasy to cook. This recipe calls for curry powder; make sure that your blend includes cumin, turmeric, coriander, chilli, black pepper, garlic and ginger.

1. Heat the oil in a large saucepan over a low heat. Add the onions, carrots and garlic. Cook for 3–4 minutes, then sprinkle over the curry powder and turmeric powder. Season with salt and pepper. Cook for a further 3–4 minutes or until the onions have softened, stirring regularly.

2. Stir in the broccoli florets and cook for 1 minute, then add the red lentils. Stir until the lentils are thoroughly mixed into the vegetables and cook for a further minute.

3. Add the canned tomatoes and stock and stir well. Increase the heat and bring the dhal to the boil, then reduce the heat to a very low simmer. Cook for 15–20 minutes on a low heat. Stir the dhal regularly and keep checking the lentils. They will swell up and become slightly translucent and begin to break apart. You can test a small spoonful to make sure the lentils are thoroughly cooked through.

4. When the dhal is ready, remove from the heat and heap into two bowls.

SERVES 2

2 tablespoons vegetable oil
2 medium onions (160g/5¾oz), chopped
2 medium carrots (160g/5¾oz), peeled and diced
2 garlic cloves, chopped
1 teaspoon curry powder
½ teaspoon ground turmeric
160g (5¾oz) broccoli florets
160g (5¾oz) dried red lentils (see Tip)
160g (5¾oz) canned tomatoes
800ml (1½ pints) vegetable stock (page 114)
salt and freshly ground black pepper, to taste

TIP: *If you're following a low FODMAP diet, soak the lentils overnight prior to cooking.*

Butternut, chestnut & brandy soup

Per serving 318 kcals | 9.3g fat | 1.1g saturates | 45.9g carbohydrates | 4.9g protein | 19.8g sugars
Vitamins A & C, Folate & Potassium

This is another festive soup, and a great way of using up any leftover veg we might have during the holiday season. We've opted for nutmeg and ginger to season, as they pair well with the sweetness of brandy. If your mulled-wine sessions have consumed all your nutmeg stores, you could always opt for allspice or cloves. The parsnip crisps will bring your total vegetable count to 5, and are a proven favourite with picky eaters.

1. Heat the oil in a large saucepan over a low heat. Add the onion, squash, carrots, sweet potato, nutmeg and ginger. Season with salt and pepper and cook for 5–7 minutes, stirring regularly, until the onions turn translucent and the vegetables have begun to soften.

2. Pour in the vegetable stock, increase the heat and bring the soup to a boil for 30 seconds. Reduce the heat to a simmer for a further 3 minutes.

3. Add the chestnuts to the soup along with the brandy and simmer for a further 2 minutes.

4. Take off the heat and blend with a hand blender or in a food processor until completely smooth. Serve with the parsnip crisps and enjoy this gem of a soup!

SERVES 2

1 tablespoon vegetable oil
2 medium onions (160g/5¾oz), chopped
160g (5¾oz) butternut squash, peeled, deseeded and chopped into chunks
2 medium carrots (160g/5¾oz), peeled and chopped
1 medium sweet potato (160g/5¾oz), peeled and chopped
½ teaspoon ground nutmeg
½ teaspoon ground ginger
500ml (18fl oz) vegetable stock (page 114)
50g (1¾oz) pre-cooked vacuum-packed chestnuts, roughly chopped
2 teaspoons brandy
salt and freshly ground black pepper

To serve
parsnip crisps (page 124)

Courgette & yellow split pea soup

Per serving 423 kcals | 14g fat | 1.3g saturates | 44.2g carbohydrates | 19.5g protein | 11.4g sugars
Vitamins C, B1 & B6, Folate, Potassium, Phosphorus, Iron & Manganese

Starchy yellow split peas in this dish make for a wondrously thick and filling soup, perfect for the colder months. They are a plant-based powerhouse chock full of protein and vitamin B1, which helps our body convert the food we eat into energy, essential for the maintenance of our metabolism and nervous system.

1. Heat the oil in a medium-sized saucepan over a low heat. Add the leeks and garlic and cook for 2–3 minutes.

2. Now add the courgettes, carrots, broccoli and parsley. Season with salt and pepper, stir to combine and cook for a further 3–5 minutes or until the vegetables begin to soften.

3. Add the yellow split peas and stir them into the vegetables for 30 seconds. Pour over the vegetable stock and stir well. Increase the heat and bring the soup to the boil, then reduce the heat to a low simmer for 10–15 minutes, stirring regularly to make sure nothing is sticking to the base of the pan.

4. The yellow split peas should be completely soft and slightly breaking apart. If not, cook for up to another 5 minutes. If necessary, add a bit more stock to make sure there is enough liquid.

5. Take the soup off the heat and blend with a hand blender or in a food processor until smooth. Divide between two bowls and serve piping hot topped with parsley and with a side of crusty bread. Enjoy!

SERVES 2

2 tablespoons vegetable oil
1 medium leek (160g/5¾oz), trimmed and chopped
1 garlic clove, finely chopped
1½ courgettes (160g/5¾oz), chopped
2 medium carrots (160g/5¾oz), peeled and chopped
160g (5¾oz) broccoli florets
handful of freshly chopped parsley, plus extra to serve
160g (5¾oz) dried yellow split peas
750ml (1⅓ pints) vegetable stock (page 114)
salt and freshly ground black pepper, to taste

Tomato melanzane soup

Per serving 286 kcals | 17g fat | 1.2g saturates | 23.8g carbohydrates | 4.5g protein | 20.4g sugars
Vitamins A, C, E & B6, Folate & Potassium

For a taste of Italy on a cold winter's evening, this soup is just the ticket! Melanzane (pronounced mel-ann-zan-eh) is the Italian for aubergine, and they form a crucial part of this dish. Aubergines provide us with so many health benefits, but they are often overlooked. We can never have too much purple in our diets, so give this versatile veg a go!

1. Heat the oil in a medium saucepan over a low heat. Add the onions, red peppers and carrots. Cook for 3–4 minutes, stirring occasionally.

2. Now add the aubergine and basil, and season with salt and pepper. Stir to combine, then cook for 4–5 minutes until the onions have softened and are starting to turn golden brown.

3. Add the tomatoes and stir. Cook for 1 minute, then pour in the vegetable stock. Increase the heat and bring the soup to the boil, then reduce the heat to a simmer for 5–7 minutes.

4. Take off the heat and blend with a hand blender or in a food processor until smooth. Top with some fresh basil, if desired, then serve. Enjoy!

SERVES 2

2 tablespoons vegetable oil
2 medium onions (160g/5¾oz), chopped
2 red peppers (160g/5¾oz), deseeded and chopped
2 medium carrots (160g/5¾oz), peeled and chopped
1 large aubergine (160g/5¾oz), diced
large handful of fresh basil, plus extra to serve (optional)
160g (5¾oz) canned tomatoes
600ml (20floz) vegetable stock (page 114)
salt and freshly ground black pepper, to taste

Tuscan bean soup

Per serving 395 kcals | 14g fat | 2.1g saturates | 47.6g carbohydrates | 12.6g protein | 14.2g sugars
Vitamins A & B1, Folate & Potassium

This soup is thick, filling and comforting, with a delicate fragrance from the rosemary. The fabulously creamy borlotti bean is packed full of fibre for optimal digestive health and is a fantastic source of plant-based protein. Serve with some delicious artisanal bread drizzled with a splash of olive oil for the perfect Mediterranean dinner.

1. Heat the oil in a large saucepan over a low heat. Add the onions, carrots, courgettes and garlic. Cook for 5 minutes. Add the rosemary, season with salt and pepper and cook for up to 5 more minutes, or until the onions are soft and translucent.

2. Add the tomato purée and the borlotti beans, along with their juice. Stir to combine with the vegetables. Cook for 2–3 minutes.

3. Now add the dried pasta and mix in for a minute. Pour in the vegetable stock. Increase the heat and bring the soup to the boil, then reduce the heat to low and simmer for 10–15 minutes. Check the pasta to make sure it is cooked.

4. Taste for seasoning and remove from the heat. Pour half of the soup into a blender and blend until smooth. Add the puréed soup back into the pan on a low heat, stirring to combine and reheat.

5. Generously fill two bowls with the bean soup and serve with crusty bread. Top with some vegan cheese, if you wish. Serve and enjoy!

SERVES 2

2 tablespoons olive oil
2 medium onions (160g/5¾oz), chopped
2 medium carrots (160g/5¾oz), peeled and chopped
1½ courgettes (160g/5¾oz), chopped
2 garlic cloves, minced
1 tablespoon freshly chopped rosemary
3 tablespoons double-concentrated tomato purée
2 x 400g (14oz) cans borlotti beans (do not drain)
100g (3½oz) dried soup pasta, such as orzo, stellette or bucato
650ml (1¼ pints) vegetable stock (page 114)
salt and freshly ground black pepper, to taste
crusty bread, to serve (optional)
vegan hard cheese, to serve (optional)

Brussels sprouts & chestnut soup

Per serving 378 kcals | 15g fat | 1.5g saturates | 46.3g carbohydrates | 7.6g protein | 28.8g sugars
Vitamins A, C, B1 & B6, Folate, Potassium & Manganese

This soup combines the colours of the festive season with the flavours and the fun! The Brussels lend a creamy texture to the soup and, although we know they're a divisive vegetable, you could serve this soup while people try to guess what's in it. By the time the soup is blended, the Brussels sprouts flavour is hardly noticeable. Instead, it's the pop of cranberry that gives the soup its kick. Serve with parsnip crisps (page 124) to reach your 5 a day and add some delicious crunch.

1. Heat the oil in a medium-sized saucepan over a low heat and add the onions. Cook for 3–4 minutes, then stir in the garlic and nutmeg. Cook for a further 3–4 minutes, or until the onions are lightly caramelized.

2. Add the Brussels sprouts, spinach and chestnuts. Cook for 5 minutes, or until the sprouts have softened and the spinach has wilted.

3. Pour in the vegetable stock. Increase the heat and bring the soup to the boil for 1 minute. Reduce the heat to a simmer for another 5 minutes.

4. Take off the heat and blend with a hand blender or in a food processor until smooth.

5. Now add the cranberries and lightly blend a little more until the cranberries are roughly chopped. Serve with the parsnip crisps.

SERVES 2

2 tablespoons vegetable oil
2 medium onions (160g/5¾oz), chopped
1 garlic clove, chopped
½ teaspoon ground nutmeg
160g (5¾oz) Brussels sprouts, trimmed and sliced
160g (5¾oz) spinach, fresh or frozen
35g pre-cooked vacuum-packed chestnuts, chopped
700ml (1¼ pints) vegetable stock
60g (2¼oz) dried cranberries
salt and freshly ground black pepper, to taste
parsnip crisps, to serve (page 124)

Thai green curry soup

Per serving 337 kcals | 24g fat | 5.1g saturates | 13.6g carbohydrates | 11.1g protein | 11.2g sugars
Vitamins C, B1, B2, B3, B6 & E, Folate, Potassium, Phosphorus, Magnesium & Iron

Curry: a classic comfort food, and so quick and easy to make! I find the smoky, earthy taste of shiitake mushrooms works beautifully when accompanied by glorious green vegetables and luscious coconut cream in this curry.

1. Heat the oil in a medium-sized saucepan over a low heat and stir in the green beans, shallots or onions, mushrooms, green peppers and broccoli. Cook for 3–4 minutes to soften slightly.

2. Add the ginger, chilli and curry paste. Cook for a few minutes more, until the mushrooms have shrunk and released some water.

3. Add the vegetable stock, coconut cream and lemon juice. Season to taste. Let the whole dish simmer on a low heat for a further 5–10 minutes, stirring frequently, until it reaches your desired consistency.

4. Take off the heat and serve in a bowl, topped with the cooked rice.

SERVES 1

1 tablespoon vegetable oil

80g (2¾oz) green beans, trimmed and chopped

1 shallot or medium onion (80g/2¾oz), chopped

80g (2¾oz) shiitake mushrooms, chopped

80g (2¾oz) green pepper, deseeded and chopped

80g (2¾oz) long stem broccoli, chopped

1 teaspoon grated fresh ginger

¼– ½ green chilli, deseeded and chopped

1 tablespoon vegan-friendly Thai green curry paste

150ml (¼ pint) vegetable stock (page 114)

20ml (¾floz) coconut cream

1 teaspoon lemon juice

40g (1½oz) cooked basmati rice

salt and freshly ground black pepper, to taste

Spiced pineapple & tomato soup

Per serving 469 kcals | 18g fat | 1.4g saturates | 56.4g carbohydrates | 11.9g protein | 26.3g sugars
Vitamins A, C, E, B1 & B6, Folate, Potassium, Iron, Copper & Manganese

We were looking for a way to squeeze some pineapple into one of the dishes and thus, this sweet and spiced dish was born! Pineapple is notably packed with manganese, which benefits our metabolism, and vitamin C, which aids our absorption of iron. If you like a bit of heat in your life, add the chilli – it makes for a perfect pick-me-up.

1. Preheat the oven to 200°C/180°C fan/400°F/gas mark 6.

2. Spread out the pineapple, tomatoes, sweet potatoes, red peppers, onions, chickpeas and garlic on a baking tray in an even layer. Drizzle with the oil, then sprinkle over the herbs and ground spices. Season with salt and pepper and mix until all the vegetables are fully coated.

3. Roast for 40 minutes, stirring halfway through.

4. Remove from the oven and discard the bay leaves. Transfer a third of the vegetables into a food processor and add the lime juice, vegetable stock and chilli (if using). Blend until smooth.

5. Mix the remaining roasted vegetables into the purée and check for seasoning. Divide between two bowls and serve. Enjoy!

SERVES 2

160g (5¾oz) fresh pineapple, peeled and chopped

160g (5¾oz) cherry tomatoes, left whole

1 medium sweet potato (160g/5¾oz), peeled and cubed

2 red peppers (160g/5¾oz), deseeded and chopped

2 medium onions (160g/5¾oz), chopped

60g (2¼oz) canned chickpeas

2 garlic cloves, chopped

2 tablespoons vegetable oil

1 tablespoon dried thyme

2 bay leaves

1 teaspoon ground cinnamon

½ teaspoon ground allspice

2 teaspoons fresh lime juice

400ml (14floz) vegetable stock (page 114)

¼ —½ fresh red chilli, deseeded and chopped (optional)

salt and freshly ground black pepper, to taste

Jerusalem artichoke & parsnip soup

Per serving 432 kcals | 26g fat | 2.6g saturates | 38.8g carbohydrates | 6g protein | 23.3g sugars
Vitamins A, C, B1 & E, Folate & Potassium

It's fair to say that Jerusalem artichokes aren't the most enticing of vegetables when it comes to looks! Nevertheless, it's all about the taste – and the many health benefits that this creamy root vegetable offers. Jerusalem artichokes contain inulin, a prebiotic that our body does not digest. Inulin is a food source for the 'good' probiotic organisms that are found in our bodies. This can help prevent the build-up of 'bad' bacteria and aid in the digestive process. A super-charged soup that tastes great whilst simultaneously nourishing your gut!

1. Heat the oil in a medium-sized saucepan over a low heat. Add the onions and cook for 2–3 minutes, stirring regularly.

2. Add the Jerusalem artichokes, parsnips, carrots, garlic and parsley. Season with salt and pepper and cook for a further 5 minutes on a low heat until the vegetables begin to soften.

3. Pour in the vegetable stock. Increase the heat and bring the soup to the boil, then reduce to a simmer for 5–7 minutes, or until the vegetables are soft.

4. Remove from the heat and blend with a hand blender or in a food processor until completely smooth. Divide between two bowls and drizzle over the truffle oil, if using. Top with spiced chickpeas to hit your 5 a day, or parsnip crisps to get an extra parsnip kick.

SERVES 2

2 tablespoons vegetable oil
2 medium onions (160g/5¾oz), chopped
2 large Jerusalem artichokes (160g/5¾oz), peeled and chopped
2 medium parsnips (160g/5¾oz), peeled and chopped
2 medium carrots (160g/5¾oz), peeled and chopped
2 garlic cloves, chopped
handful of freshly chopped parsley
500ml (18floz) vegetable stock (page 114)
salt and freshly ground black pepper, to taste
1–2 tablespoons truffle oil (optional)

To serve
spiced chickpeas (see page 123) or parsnip crisps (see page 124)

Cauliflower, rosemary & lavender soup

Per serving 335 kcals | 17g fat | 1.4g saturates | 31.7g carbohydrates | 6.6g protein | 20.5g sugars
Vitamins A, C, B1 & B6, Folate & Potassium

This soup has such a delicious flavour. Rosemary and lavender make a fabulous pairing and they really complement the roasted veg perfectly. This soup is best when it's silky smooth, so it is worth the extra time blending to get it just right. There are so many toppings and accompaniments that go perfectly with this dish, but here we've used the spiced chickpeas on page 123.

1. Preheat the oven to 200°C/180°C fan/400°F/gas mark 6.

2. Place the cauliflower, parsnips and swede on a baking tray and scatter over the rosemary and lavender, along with some salt and pepper. Drizzle with the oil and toss together. Spread out on the tray in an even layer and roast in the oven for 15–20 minutes, or until just starting to brown at the edges.

3. Remove from the oven and add the onions and garlic to the tray. Return to the oven and roast for another 10–15 minutes, or until roasted but not burnt. Keep an eye on the oven, as you don't want the vegetables to char.

4. Tip all the roasted vegetables into a food processor and pour in the lemon juice and vegetable stock. Blend until completely smooth, then place in a saucepan over a medium heat to warm through. Divide between two bowls and serve topped with the spiced chickpeas.

SERVES 2

160g (5¾oz) cauliflower florets
2 parsnips (160g/5¾oz), peeled and chopped
160g (5¾oz) swede, peeled and chopped
2 teaspoons fresh rosemary, or 1 teaspoon dried
1–2 teaspoons dried lavender
2 tablespoons vegetable oil
2 medium onions (160g/5¾oz), chopped
2 garlic cloves, chopped
1 teaspoon lemon juice
750ml (1⅓ pints) vegetable stock (page 114)
salt and freshly ground black pepper, to taste
spiced chickpeas (see page 123), to serve

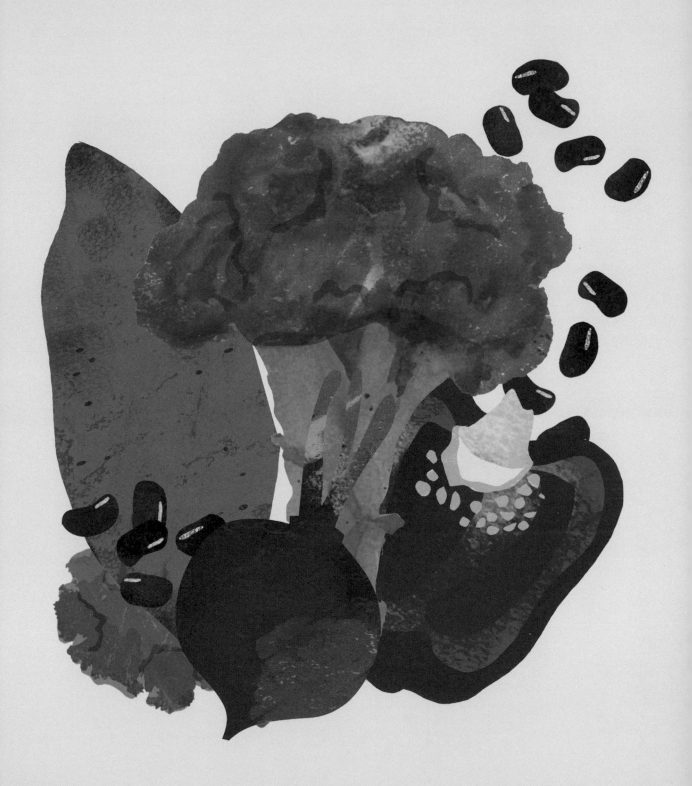

bowl food

Tagliatelle with olive & sundried tomato tapenade

Per serving 219 kcals | 10g fat | 1.2g saturates | 19.1g carbohydrates | 6.9g protein | 16g sugars
Vitamins C, B1 & B6, Folate & Potassium

Italy meets France in this healthy Mediterranean-inspired dish, with a filling pasta base and chunky tapenade. This isn't your run-of-the-mill pasta dish! Once all the vegetables are together, even people who are a bit funny about olives will be delighted by the flavour.

1. Mix together the mushrooms, olives and tomatoes. Cook the tagliatelle according to the packet instructions.

2. Meanwhile, heat the oil in a medium-sized saucepan over a low heat and add the onion and garlic. Cook for 4–5 minutes.

3. Season with salt and pepper, then sprinkle over the fresh basil. Now add the mushroom, olive and tomato mixture to the saucepan. Cook for a further 5–6 minutes, stirring regularly.

4. Squeeze in the tomato purée and stir. Add the fresh spinach and mix to combine until the spinach has wilted.

5. Drain the pasta (see Tip) and add it to the tapenade. Mix well to thoroughly coat the pasta in the vegetables.

6. Divide between two bowls and serve topped with some more fresh basil and a scattering of toasted pine nuts and Parmesan-style cheese, if using.

SERVES 2

160g (5¾oz) portobello mushrooms, finely diced
160g (5¾oz) green olives, pitted and finely diced
80g (2¾oz) sundried tomatoes, finely diced
150g (5⅓oz) dried tagliatelle
2 tablespoons vegetable oil
2 medium red onions (160g/5¾oz), finely chopped
2 garlic cloves, finely chopped
handful of freshly chopped basil, plus extra to serve
2 tablespoons double-concentrated tomato purée
160g (5¾oz) fresh spinach
salt and freshly ground black pepper, to taste
handful of toasted pine nuts, to serve (optional)
Parmesan-style cheese, to serve (optional)

TIP: *If you prefer a consistency that's more like sauce than tapenade, you can take a few tablespoons of the pasta water and add it to the vegetable mixture to thin it out.*

Noodle Buddha bowl

*Per serving 562 kcals | 11g fat | 1.2g saturates | 48.4g carbohydrates | 23.7g protein | 14.2g sugars
Vitamins A, C & B1, Folate, Potassium & Manganese*

This is a Buddha bowl with a twist: the peach dressing gives it a fresh, zingy taste and just screams summer. Tasty tofu is all about the marinade, as it happily absorbs flavours. If you like to eat seasonally (check out the seasonality chart on page 11) you could substitute some of the vegetables depending on what's available.

1. Preheat your oven to 240°C/220°C fan/475°F/gas mark 9 and line a baking tray with baking paper.

2. Place the tofu between a few sheets of kitchen roll. Squeeze it gently until a good amount of liquid has come out, then transfer the tofu to a chopping board and cut into 2-cm (1-inch) cubes.

3. Combine the marinade ingredients in small bowl. Add the tofu and stir it around until fully coated.

4. Lay the tofu out in a single layer on the prepared baking tray. Drizzle over any leftover marinade and bake in the oven for 15 minutes until browned.

5. Meanwhile, add all the peach dressing ingredients to a blender. Season with salt and pepper and blend until completely smooth.

6. When everything is ready, place the noodles in a large bowl. Arrange the edamame beans, beetroot, tomatoes, mango and baked tofu on top. Drizzle over your peach dressing, serve and enjoy!

SERVES 1

130g (4½oz) tofu

For the marinade
1 tablespoon tamari
¼ teaspoon grated ginger
1 garlic clove, grated
1 teaspoon maple syrup
salt and freshly ground black
   pepper, to taste

For the vegetables
60g (2¼oz) noodles, cooked
   according to packet
   instructions
80g (2¾oz) edamame beans
80g (2¾oz) cooked beetroot
   chunks
80g (2¾oz) cherry tomatoes,
   halved
80g (2¾oz) mango chunks

For the peach dressing
1 tablespoon white wine
   vinegar
½ tablespoon tamari
1 tablespoon olive oil
½ teaspoon grated fresh
   ginger
½ teaspoon grated garlic
1 peach (80g/2¾oz), quartered

Creamy leek and sweetcorn risotto

Per serving 458 kcals | 17g fat | 4.8g saturates | 54.7g carbohydrates | 16.9g protein | 8.7g sugars
Vitamins A, C, B1, B2, B3, B6 & B12, Folate, Potassium, Zinc & Manganese

This risotto makes quite a lot for two people, as it's loaded with a grand variety of vegetables that all contribute to your 5 a day. Avid meal preppers will rejoice to hear that this dish is great for eating half a portion at lunch and half at dinner.

1. Heat the oil in a large saucepan over a low heat. Add the leeks and garlic and cook for 3–4 minutes. Sprinkle in the basil and nutritional yeast and season with salt and pepper. Cook for a further 3–4 minutes or until the leeks are soft, stirring occasionally.

2. Add the sweetcorn, chickpeas and spinach. Cook for a couple of minutes – this step might take a few minutes longer if you are using frozen spinach as you need it to have thawed slightly before moving on.

3. Tip in the risotto rice. Stir and cook for 1 minute.

4. Add the tomatoes and cook for another minute. Now pour in the vegetable stock. Bring the risotto to a simmer and cook, stirring regularly, for 10–15 minutes. Keep checking the rice to make sure it cooks through.

5. When the rice is almost cooked, add the lemon juice and coconut cream. Stir and warm it through, taste for seasoning, then serve.

SERVES 2

1½ tablespoons vegetable oil
1–2 leeks (160g/5¾oz), trimmed and chopped
2 garlic cloves, finely chopped
handful of freshly chopped basil
1 tablespoon nutritional yeast
160g (5¾oz) sweetcorn, frozen or canned
160g (5¾oz) canned chickpeas, drained
160g (5¾oz) spinach, fresh or frozen
80g (2¾oz) risotto rice
160g (5¾oz) canned tomatoes
300ml–400ml (10–14floz) vegetable stock (page 114)
2 teaspoons lemon juice
2 tablespoons coconut cream
salt and freshly ground black pepper, to taste

Chana masala

*Per serving 219 kcals | 10g fat | 1.2g saturates | 19.1g carbohydrates | 6.9g protein | 16g sugars
Vitamins C, B1 & B6, Folate & Potassium*

Chana masala used to be the only choice on the menu for hard-pressed vegans eating out. However, this 5 a day reworking of the classic recipe will make you rethink the whole thing! I like to serve it on a bed of rice with some steamed broccoli, a dollop of vegan yogurt and naan bread.

1. Heat the oil in a medium-sized saucepan over a low heat. Add the onion, garlic and ginger and cook for 5 minutes, stirring regularly.

2. Add the chilli, cinnamon stick, coriander, curry powder and turmeric. Stir to thoroughly mix in the spices and cook for a few more minutes, or until the onion is soft and the aroma of spices has filled your kitchen.

3. Now add in the chickpeas and stir to combine. Cook for a further minute, stirring occasionally.

4. Season with salt and pepper. Add the tinned tomatoes and mango chutney and mix well. Cook for 1 minute more, then slowly add the spinach, a handful at a time. Allow the spinach to wilt with each addition, stirring it into the chickpeas, until it has all been combined.

5. Cook for 5–10 minutes on a low heat or until the chana masala reaches your desired consistency.

6. Serve between two bowls on a bed of rice with some steamed broccoli, a dollop of vegan yogurt, naan bread and a sprinkle of fresh coriander. Enjoy!

SERVES 2

1 tablespoon vegetable or coconut oil
2 medium onions (160g/5¾oz), diced
2 garlic cloves, minced
½ teaspoon grated fresh ginger
¼ –½ red chilli, finely chopped
1 cinnamon stick
½ teaspoon ground coriander
½ teaspoon curry powder
¼ teaspoon ground turmeric
1 x 400g (14oz) can chickpeas, drained
200g (7oz) canned tomatoes
1 tablespoon mango chutney
160g (5¾oz) baby spinach
salt and freshly ground black pepper

To serve
cooked basmati rice
160g (5¾oz) steamed broccoli
plain vegan yogurt
naan bread

Sweet potato & cherry tomato roast

Per serving 589 kcals | 38g fat | 5.5g saturates | 40.5g carbohydrates | 13.7g protein | 21.5g sugars
Vitamins A, C, B1, B2, B3, B6 & B12, Folate, Potassium, Calcium, Magnesium, Iron & Zinc

This dish is sweet, crispy and bursting with fresh flavours, with minimal washing-up afterwards. The inclusion of the tofu 'egg' might seem tricky, but you'll be basking in your culinary glory when you pull this off!

1. Preheat your oven to 240°C/220°C fan/475°F/gas mark 9 and line a baking tray with baking paper.

2. Place the sweet potatoes in a large bowl. Drizzle over the olive oil, dried oregano, basil and paprika, if using. Season with salt and pepper. Toss together to coat the sweet potato in the herbs and spices.

3. Lay the sweet potato wedges out on the prepared tray in an even layer, setting the bowl aside. Roast for 20 minutes.

4. Meanwhile, mix together the carrots, onions, red pepper and tomatoes in the same bowl you previously used for the sweet potato. Toss the vegetables around the bowl to pick up any leftover oil and herbs.

5. If you're making the tofu egg, follow the instructions on page 129.

6. Remove the sweet potato from the oven. Add the other vegetables to the baking tray and use a spatula to spread them out. If using the tofu 'egg', make two gaps amongst the vegetables to place the rounds of tofu flat on the tray. Lastly, crumble the vegan cheese all over the dish (if using) and sprinkle with the fresh parsley. Add an extra sprinkle of salt and pepper over the whole tray.

SERVES 2

For the sweet potato mixture
1 medium sweet potato
   (160g/5¾oz), peeled and cut
   into large wedges
4 teaspoons olive oil
1 teaspoon dried oregano
1 teaspoon dried basil, or 1
   handful of chopped fresh
¼ teaspoon sweet paprika
   (optional)
2 medium carrots
   (160g/5¾oz), peeled and
   chopped into large chunks
2 medium red onions
   (160g/5¾oz), chopped into
   large chunks
160g (5¾oz) red pepper,
   deseeded and chopped into
   small cubes
160g (5¾oz) fresh cherry
   tomatoes, halved
2 x tofu eggs (page 129)
70g (2½oz) feta-style vegan
   cheese (optional)
handful of freshly chopped flat-
   leaf parsley
salt and freshly ground black
   pepper

For the tahini dressing
4 tablespoons tahini paste
1 tablespoon fresh lime juice
1 tablespoon maple syrup
2 teaspoons olive oil
½ teaspoon Dijon mustard
   (check the label for sulphites
   as these are not vegan) or
   English-style mustard
1 tablespoon cold water
1 teaspoon poppy seeds
   (optional)

7. Return to the oven for a further 10 minutes. Meanwhile, make the tahini dressing. Place all the ingredients in a medium bowl and season with salt and pepper. Whisk together until the dressing turns smooth and creamy. Taste for seasoning.

8. Once cooked, remove the vegetables from the oven. Divide them between two plates, placing a tofu 'egg' (if using) on each. Now, drizzle the tahini dressing over everything and savour every mouthful – enjoy!

Mac & 'cheese'

Per serving 219 kcals | 10g fat | 1.2g saturates | 19.1g carbohydrates | 6.9g protein | 16g sugars
Vitamins A C, B1, B2, B3, B6 & B12, Folate, Biotin, Potassium, Zinc & Manganese

This is a delicious, comforting meal that really radiates that Friday feeling. It's also perfect to rustle up at the end of the week if you're thinking about giving your fridge or freezer a bit of a clear out. The 'cheese' sauce is rich and creamy, and the nutritional yeast provides the scrumptious cheesy taste.

1. Begin by bringing a small saucepan of water to the boil over a medium heat. Add the carrots and sweet potatoes, then simmer for about 10 minutes or until the vegetables are soft.

2. In the meantime, bring a larger saucepan of water to the boil over a medium heat. Add the pasta and cook according to the packet instructions. For the last 5 minutes of the pasta's cooking time, drop in the cauliflower florets, sweetcorn and spinach.

3. In a bowl, mix together the nutritional yeast, onion granules, garlic powder, vegetable oil, lemon juice and vegetable stock. Season with salt and pepper.

4. Drain the carrots and sweet potatoes and return to the pan. Tip the nutritional yeast mixture into the saucepan and use a hand blender to blend the ingredients until thoroughly smooth and creamy. Alternatively, you could pour the mixture into a food processor to blend until smooth.

5. Drain the pasta and vegetable mixture. Pour the creamy 'cheese' sauce on top and stir well. Taste for seasoning then divide generously between two bowls. Top with your favourite vegan cheese, then serve.

SERVES 2

2 medium carrots (160g/5¾oz), peeled and diced
1 medium sweet potato (160g/5¾oz), peeled and diced
130g (4½oz) dried macaroni
160g (5¾oz) cauliflower florets, fresh or frozen
160g (5¾oz) sweetcorn, fresh or frozen
160g (5¾oz) spinach, fresh or frozen
1 tablespoon nutritional yeast
1 teaspoon onion granules
½ teaspoon garlic powder
2 tablespoons vegetable oil
1 tablespoon lemon juice
125ml (4floz) vegetable stock
salt and freshly ground black pepper, to taste
vegan cheese, to serve (page 114)

Cauliflower & pineapple poke bowl

Per serving 462 kcals | 23g fat | 1.8g saturates | 44.3g carbohydrates | 13.2g protein | 25.7g sugars
Vitamins A, C, E, B1 & B6, Folate, Potassium & Manganese

Poke (pronounced poh-kay) bowls originate from Hawaii, and the word means 'to slice'. Traditionally, this dish would have featured diced fish, usually raw. However, it's now become an exciting way of creating and serving wonderfully fragrant and colourful combinations of the freshest of foods served in a bowl. This dish is light, yet powerfully nutritious. It's easy to adapt and vary according to your tastes.

1. Preheat the oven to 200°C/180°C fan/400°F/gas mark 6.

2. Put all the vegetables and the pineapple on a baking tray and drizzle with the oil. Season with salt and pepper. Mix the vegetables around until they are fully coated, then spread them out in an even layer.

3. Roast for 25 minutes, or until the vegetables turn golden.

4. Meanwhile, cook the rice according to the packet instructions.

5. When you're ready to serve, place the cooked rice in a bowl. Spoon the roasted vegetables over the rice. Pour the tamari over the top, then serve and enjoy!

SERVES 1

1 medium carrot (80g/2¾oz), peeled and diced
80g (2¾oz) mangetout or green beans
80g (2¾oz) cauliflower florets
80g (2¾oz) canned sweetcorn, drained
80g (2¾oz) fresh pineapple, peeled and chopped
1 tablespoon vegetable oil
30g (1oz) jasmine rice
10ml (2 teaspoons) tamari
salt and freshly ground black pepper, to taste

Carrot bourguignon

Per serving 437 kcals | 10g fat | 1.1g saturates | 46g carbohydrates | 23.1g protein | 19.5g sugars
Vitamins A, B1, B2, B3, B6 & B12, Potassium, Zinc, Copper & Manganese

The fine aromas and exquisite taste of this dish will be transporting you to a rustic villa in Burgundy in no time! This recipe calls for red miso, which hails from Japan, and like many other fermented foods, is a great source of vitamin B12. If you're feeling like a soup-er star and want 6 a day, serve with mashed sweet potato instead.

1. Heat the oil in a medium, heavy-based saucepan over a low heat. Add the 'beef' or 'chicken', carrots, onion and garlic. Cook for 5 minutes until the 'meat' starts to brown and the vegetables have slightly softened. Sprinkle over the herbs and spices and season with salt and pepper. Stir well and cook for another 5 minutes.

2. Now pour in the maple syrup, liquid smoke (if using), garlic powder and nutritional yeast. Stir well to combine. Continue to cook for 5–7 minutes or until the 'meat' has reached your desired colour.

3. Add the beans, tomato purée and red miso paste (if using) and stir to combine. Now pour in the red wine and vegetable stock and stir again.

4. Increase the heat and bring to the boil, then reduce the heat to a very low simmer. Partially cover with a lid and keep at a low simmer for up to 1 hour. You want the liquid to reduce by about half and to form a syrupy-glaze texture. Check it regularly and give it a stir to stop any vegetables from sticking to the bottom of the pan.

5. About 10 minutes before the stew is ready, melt the vegan butter in a saucepan over a low heat. Add the mushrooms and cook for 5–7 minutes until they have

SERVES 2

1 tablespoon vegetable oil

2 vegan 'beef' or 'chicken' steaks cut into 5-cm (2-inch) chunks

2 large carrots (160g/5¾oz), sliced into 1-cm (½-inch) rounds

2 medium onions (160g/5¾oz), diced

3 garlic cloves, chopped

1 teaspoon finely chopped fresh thyme

handful of fresh parsley

handful of fresh sage

1 teaspoon finely chopped fresh rosemary

¼ teaspoon ground allspice

1 tablespoon maple syrup

1 tablespoon liquid smoke (optional)

1 teaspoon garlic powder

1 tablespoon nutritional yeast

160g (5¾oz) canned adzuki or pinto beans

40g (1½oz) double-concentrated tomato purée

1 teaspoon red miso paste (optional)

100ml (3½floz) red wine

250ml (9floz) vegetable stock
  (page 114)
salt and freshly ground black
  pepper

To serve
2 tablespoons vegan butter
**160g (5¾oz) portobello
  or chestnut mushrooms,
  chopped**
rice, mashed potatoes or
  noodles

reduced in size. Season with salt and pepper. Continue cooking until most of the water from the mushrooms has evaporated and you are left with a buttery mushroom mixture.

6. Remove the bourguignon from the heat. Tip in the mushrooms and stir briefly to just combine. Taste for seasoning.

7. Serve while piping hot. Savour and enjoy – it's worth the wait!

Lentil spaghetti with peas & leeks

*Per serving 590 kcals | 22g fat | 2.2g saturates | 57.6g carbohydrates | 33.1g protein | 11g sugars
Vitamins C, B1 & B6, Folate & Potassium*

Those of us on plant-based diets are more than used to hearing the question: 'But where do you get your protein from?' Rather than rolling your eyes, we suggest cooking up this dish. It should answer all and any questions about your protein intake, plus the lentil pasta also counts as one serving of your 5 a day.

1. Heat the oil in a medium-sized saucepan over a low heat. Add the leeks and garlic, cooking for 5–10 minutes or until the leeks are soft. Sprinkle over the parsley and season with salt and pepper.

2. Add the mushrooms and cook for a further 5 minutes or until the juices have seeped out of the mushrooms and are starting to evaporate. Now you can add the peas and asparagus.

3. Cook for another 5–10 minutes, or until the asparagus has softened. Add the lemon zest and juice and stir well. Pour in the cream and vegetable stock, stirring.

4. Bring the sauce to a simmer for up to 10 minutes, or until all the vegetables are cooked and the sauce has thickened slightly.

5. Meanwhile, cook the lentil spaghetti according to the packet instructions, then drain.

6. Taste the sauce for seasoning, then add the lentil spaghetti to the pan, tossing to coat it in the sauce.

7. Divide between two bowls and serve, topped with fresh parsley and a grating of your favourite vegan cheese, if you wish.

SERVES 2

1½ tablespoons vegetable oil
1 large leek (160g/5¾oz), chopped
2 garlic cloves, finely chopped
handful of freshly chopped parsley, plus extra to serve
160g (5¾oz) chestnut mushrooms, sliced
160g (5¾oz) peas, fresh or frozen
160g (5¾oz) asparagus, trimmed and chopped
zest of 1 lemon and juice of ½ lemon
150ml (¼ pint) vegan single cream
100ml (3½floz) vegetable stock (page 114)
160g (5¾oz) dried lentil spaghetti
salt and freshly ground black pepper, to taste
vegan Parmesan-style cheese (optional), to serve

TIP: *As with many of the other sauces in this book, you could make a little extra sauce, freeze and then just defrost it whenever you want.*

fruity favourites

Turmeric, mango & coconut 'soothie'

Per serving 275 kcals | 5.7g fat | 4.1g saturates | 46.8g carbohydrates | 6.3g protein | 43.6g sugars
Vitamins A, C & B6, Folate, Potassium & Manganese

Soothies are the love child of soup and smoothies! They're a delectable kick-starter for breakfast (or indeed lunch). Curcumin, the main active ingredient in turmeric, has been linked with lowering the risk of heart disease, treating inflammation and neutralising free radicals that harm and age cells.

1. Put all the ingredients into a blender and blend until smooth.

2. Pour into a glass and enjoy as a filling breakfast soup/smoothie!

SERVES 1

80g (2¾oz) mango chunks
150ml (¼ pint) orange juice, freshly squeezed or shop-bought
1 medium carrot (80g/2¾oz)
1 banana (80g/2¾oz)
80g (2¾oz) cauliflower florets, fresh or frozen
20ml (¾oz) coconut milk
½ teaspoon freshly grated ginger
½ teaspoon ground turmeric
pinch of black pepper
100ml (3½fl oz) cold water

Banana, strawberry & spinach 'soothie'

Per serving 332 kcals | 12g fat | 2.6g saturates | 37.7g carbohydrates | 13.3g protein | 34g sugars
Vitamins A, C & B6, Folate, Potassium & Manganese

There's so much space for ingenuity and imagination here, we really just want you to have fun with it and get your 5 a day! The choice of nut or seed butter, plant milk and sweetener is entirely up to you, but if you're having this for breakfast, a protein-rich plant milk like soya will be beneficial to get you going for the day.

1. Place all the ingredients in a blender and blend until smooth.

2. Serve in a bowl and top with any of the suggestions above – or whatever else you fancy. Enjoy!

SERVES 1

80g (2¾oz) mango chunks
80g (2¾oz) spinach, fresh or frozen
80g (2¾oz) cauliflower florets, fresh or frozen
1 banana (80g/2¾oz)
80g (2¾oz) strawberries, hulled
1 tablespoon your chosen nut or seed butter
100ml (3½floz) your chosen plant milk

To serve
Your choice of granola, cereal, chopped nuts, seeds, fresh fruit or chocolate shavings

Spinach, mango & lime 'soothie'

Per serving 239 kcals | 1.6g fat | 0.3g saturates | 44.6g carbohydrates | 6.9g protein | 41.5g sugars
Vitamins A, C & B6, Folate, Potassium, Copper & Manganese

We love the combination of lime, mint and mango in this 'soothie'. It's so refreshing and cool that it reminds us of a mojito! It makes for a great boost at breakfast or an awesome alternative to ice cream in the summer. You'll get the remaining two servings of your 5 a day by serving it with some sliced banana and kiwi. Feel free to accessorize this dish however you like, with nuts, seeds or puffed grains!

1. Place all the 'soothie' ingredients in a food processor and blend until smooth. Pour out into a bowl and top with the banana and kiwi. Serve and enjoy!

SERVES 1

120g (4¼oz) fresh mango
  chunks
80g (2¾oz) fresh spinach
zest and juice of 1 lime
small handful of freshly
  chopped mint
80g (2¾oz) cauliflower, fresh
  or frozen
100ml water

To serve:
1 banana (80g/2¾oz), sliced
1 kiwi (80g/2¾oz), peeled
  and sliced

Carrot cake porridge

Per serving 438 kcals | 7.2g fat | 1.2g saturates | 77.8g carbohydrates | 10.7g protein | 54.8g sugars
Vitamins A, C & B1, Folate, Potassium, Copper & Manganese

We love this porridge. All the fruit, veg and spices create such glorious flavours and colours and it has lifted the mood of many a gloomy morning. For anyone who's not a carrot fan, we think this might be the dish that makes them a carrot convert! To meet your 5 a day, we suggest drinking fruit juice alongside this porridge.

1. Place all the porridge ingredients in a small saucepan over a medium heat. Cook, stirring occasionally, until the milk starts to bubble. Reduce the heat down and continue to cook, stirring continuously, for another 3–5 minutes or until the porridge reaches your desired consistency.

2. Take off the heat and pour the porridge out into a bowl. Top with the cubed pineapple and drizzle over the maple syrup or agave nectar.

3. Serve the porridge with a glass of fresh orange juice and savour the indulgence.

SERVES 1

30g (1oz) porridge oats
80g (2¾oz) carrot, grated
1 teaspoon ground flaxseed
½ teaspoon ground cinnamon
pinch of ground nutmeg
drop of vanilla extract
110ml (3¾floz) plant milk
110ml (3¾floz) water
1 banana (80g/2¾oz), mashed
30g (1oz) raisins or sultanas

To serve
80g (2¾oz) pineapple chunks, fresh or canned
1 teaspoon maple syrup or agave nectar
150ml (¼ pint) orange juice

Summery berry & sweetcorn soup

Per serving 299 kcals | 4.5g fat | 0.6g saturates | 45.4g carbohydrates | 11.4g protein | 37g sugars
Vitamins A, C, B1, B2, B3, B6 & C, Folate, Pantothenate Potassium & Manganese,
Calcium, Phosphorus, Magnesium, Iron, Zinc & Copper

This is an invigorating, summery raw soup that will change the way people look at berries. The sweetness of the apples and sweetcorn, as well as the refreshing taste of the cucumber, balance out any berry-related sour notes. These bountiful berries are a fantastic source of vitamin C, which contributes to healthy skin and iron absorption.

1. Place all ingredients in a blender. Season with salt and pepper to taste and blend until completely smooth. If you prefer an even smoother texture, you can sieve it.

2. Chill in the fridge for 1–2 hours.

3. Serve in a bowl with a dollop of the ricotta (if using) and a sprig of mint, if desired. Enjoy!

SERVES 1

100g (3½oz) raspberries or
  blackberries
80g (2¾oz) sweetcorn,
  canned or frozen
½ apple (80g/2¾oz), cored
  and chopped
80g (2¾oz) cucumber,
  chopped
80g (2¾oz) cauliflower florets,
  fresh or frozen
½ garlic clove
1 tablespoon freshly chopped
  basil
1 tablespoon freshly chopped
  mint, plus 1 sprig to serve
1 tablespoon maple syrup
  (optional)
salt and freshly ground black
  pepper
vegan ricotta, (optional)

Fragrant cherry, basil & mint soup

Per serving 347 kcals | 15g fat | 1.1g saturates | 38.2g carbohydrates | 11.3g protein | 25.4g sugars Vitamins A & C, Folate & Potassium

The combination of sweet cherries, refreshing mint and scented basil help make this soup magnificently fragrant! This is quite a useful recipe if you've bought some fresh basil and mint to grow on your windowsill but are unsure of how to incorporate them in both savoury and sweet dishes. The inclusion of creamy white beans bulks up the liquid and helps to bring out the piquancy of this refreshing, easy soup.

1. Heat the oil in a medium-sized saucepan over a low heat. Add the onions and cook for 2–3 minutes until slightly softened. Now add the courgette and cook for a further 2–3 minutes.

2. Add the cherries, kale, white beans, mint and basil. Stir and season with salt and pepper. Cook for another 2 minutes until everything is combined and softening.

3. Add the lemon juice and agave nectar. Stir, then pour in the vegetable stock.

4. Increase the heat and bring the soup to the boil, then reduce to a simmer for 5 minutes, partially covering the saucepan with a lid. Remove from the heat and blend until completely smooth.

5. Taste for seasoning, then serve this deliciously fragrant soup. If you prefer, you can also chill the soup for at least 3 hours and serve it cold on a summer's day.

SERVES 2

2 tablespoons vegetable oil
2 medium onions
   (160g/5¾oz), chopped
2 medium courgettes
   (160g/5¾oz), chopped
160g (5¾oz) pitted cherries
160g (5¾oz) shredded kale,
   fresh or frozen
160g (5¾oz) canned white
   beans
2 tablespoons freshly
   chopped mint
2 tablespoons freshly
   chopped basil
juice of ½ lemon
2 tablespoons agave nectar
500ml (18fl oz) vegetable
   stock (page 114)
salt and freshly ground black
   pepper, to taste

extras

Vegetable stock

Per serving 275 kcals | 5.7g fat | 4.1g saturates | 46.8g carbohydrates | 6.3g protein | 43.6g sugars
Vitamins A, C & B6, Folate, Potassium & Manganese

Many of the recipes in this book require the use of vegetable stock or bouillon. You can either use your preferred shop-bought brand, or try out the following recipe for an easy vegan broth or stock. This makes a large quantity, but it can be frozen in batches in sealed containers and defrosted as necessary.

1. Heat the oil in a large saucepan over a low heat and add the onions. Cook for a couple of minutes until they are caramelized and golden brown.

2. Add the carrots, celery and leek and cook for 4–5 minutes, stirring occasionally.

3. Add the garlic and cook for a further 1–2 minutes, then stir in the parsley, bay leaf, thyme, mustard powder, nutmeg and turmeric. Cook for 1–2 minutes more, then add the tomato purée and stir well.

4. Pour in the measured water, increase the heat and bring to the boil. Once boiling, reduce the heat and simmer the stock gently, partially covered, for 35–40 minutes, stirring occasionally.

5. Add the kombu flakes and dried mushrooms and continue to simmer, still partially covered, for another 15–20 minutes. Season to taste and take off the heat.

6. Line a sieve or colander with a muslin cloth. Strain the stock through the lined sieve into another pan or a large bowl. You should be left with a clear broth, ready to use in your chosen recipe. This will keep in the freezer for 2–3 months and in the fridge for 2–3 days.

MAKES 2.5 LITRES

2 tablespoons vegetable oil
2 medium onions, chopped
2 medium carrots, peeled and chopped
2 celery sticks, trimmed and chopped
1–2 leeks, trimmed and chopped
3 garlic cloves, peeled and chopped
large handful of freshly chopped flat-leaf parsley
1 bay leaf
1 teaspoon fresh thyme leaves
¼ teaspoon mustard powder
¼ teaspoon ground nutmeg
¼ teaspoon ground turmeric
1 tablespoon double-concentrate tomato purée
2.5 litres (4½ pints) water
½ teaspoon dried kombu (seaweed) flakes
15g (½oz) dried porcini mushrooms
salt and freshly ground black pepper, to taste

Red onion chutney

Per serving 118 kcals | 0.7g fat | 0g saturates | 22g carbohydrates | 3.2g protein | 18.5g sugars

1. Heat the olive oil in a small saucepan over a low heat, then tip in all the remaining ingredients.

2. Cook for about 30 minutes, stirring frequently to avoid any of the vegetables from burning at the base of the pan. You want it to cook and reduce down slowly. It will be ready when the mixture looks jammy. Serve!

SERVES 2

1 teaspoon olive oil
2 medium red onions (160g/5¾oz), finely chopped
160g (5¾oz) fresh cherry tomatoes, finely chopped
2 garlic cloves, finely chopped
20g (¾oz) double-concentrated tomato purée
½ teaspoon grated fresh ginger
20g (¾oz) soft brown sugar
50ml (2floz) red wine vinegar
handful of freshly chopped basil
salt and freshly ground black pepper, to taste

Quick tomato ketchup

Per serving 154 kcals | 7.7g fat | 0.5g saturates | 17.1g carbohydrates | 2.2g protein | 14.8g sugars

1. Heat the oil in a small frying pan over a low heat. Add the garlic and cook for 2–3 minutes until it just starts to turn a golden colour. Add all the other ingredients and stir.

2. Increase the heat, bring the mixture to the boil, then reduce the heat. Simmer, stirring all the while, until the ketchup reaches your desired consistency. This should take no more than 5 minutes.

3. Transfer the ketchup into a bowl, let cool and serve. The ketchup will keep for 2 days covered in the fridge.

SERVES 2

1 teaspoon vegetable oil
1 garlic clove, minced
40g (1½oz) double-concentrated tomato purée
100g (3½oz) passata
4 teaspoons soft brown sugar
3 tablespoons lime juice
$\frac{1}{8}$ teaspoon sweet paprika
½ teaspoon onion granules
½ teaspoon salt
pinch of freshly ground black pepper
150ml (¼ pint) water

TIP: *The ketchup can also be frozen in a freezer container and defrosted in the fridge over a few hours.*

Brussels sprouts crisps

Per serving 264 kcals | 18g fat | 2.1g saturates | 9.5g carbohydrates | 12.4g protein | 4.7g sugars

1. Preheat the oven to 160°C/140°C fan/325°F/gas mark 3.

2. Remove the ends of the Brussels sprouts and peel off the first few outer leaves until the sprouts are clean. Now slice them thinly into strips.

3. Put all the other ingredients in a bowl and season to taste with salt and pepper. Add the Brussels sprouts and toss to coat, then lay them out in a single layer on a baking tray. If necessary, use two baking trays.

4. Roast in the oven for 10 minutes. Remove from the oven and stir the sprouts, then return to the oven for a further 10–15 minutes. If you want to get them extra crispy, you can change the oven to the grill setting (or put them under the grill) for a further 2–5 minutes.

5. If you have been able to stop yourself from eating all the sprouts straight away, then go ahead and serve them as an accompaniment to some of our soup recipes.

SERVES 2

200g (7oz) Brussels sprouts
½ teaspoon onion granules
¼ teaspoon garlic powder
1½ tablespoons nutritional
   yeast
2 tablespoons tahini paste
juice of ½ lime
1 tablespoon vegetable oil
salt and freshly ground black
   pepper, to taste

Kale crisps

Per serving 96 kcals | 8.5g fat | 1.2g saturates | 1.1g carbohydrates | 2.7g protein | 1g sugars

1. Preheat the oven to 160°C/140°C fan/325°F/gas mark 3.

2. Put all the ingredients in a large bowl and toss to coat the kale in the seasoning. Then lay the kale out in a single layer on a baking tray.

3. Roast in the oven for 15 minutes. Remove from oven and stir the kale, then return to the oven for a further 10 minutes, or until crisp.

4. Leave to stand for 1 minute, then eat as delicious crisps or serve alongside some of our soup recipes.

SERVES 2

160g (5¾oz) kale, torn into bite-sized pieces and stalks removed
1 tablespoon olive oil
¼ teaspoon sweet smoked paprika
½ teaspoon granulated sugar (optional)
salt and freshly ground black pepper

Sweet Potato Fries

Per serving 241 kcals | 16g fat | 2.7g saturates | 19.3g carbohydrates | 1.7g protein | 4.5g sugars

1. Preheat the oven to 240°C/220°C fan/475°F/gas mark 9 and line a baking tray with baking paper.

2. Place the sweet potato pieces in a medium bowl. Add the olive oil, rosemary, thyme, sage, paprika, salt and pepper. Using your hands, toss the sweet potatoes until they are thoroughly coated in the mixture. Lay out the sweet potatoes on the prepared tray in an even layer. If they overlap, they will steam rather than roast, and they won't end up as crispy.

3. Place in the oven for 15–20 minutes. Remove from the oven and use a spatula to give the potatoes a quick stir, then return to the oven for a further 10 minutes or until nice and crispy.

4. Remove from the oven and add an extra sprinkle of sea salt flakes. Serve with the quick tomato ketchup (page 119).

SERVES 2

1 medium sweet potato (160g/5¾oz), peeled and chopped into long, thin chips (see Tip)
2 tablespoons olive oil
1 teaspoon dried rosemary
1 teaspoon dried thyme
1 teaspoon dried sage
¼ teaspoon sweet paprika
a couple of pinches of sea salt flakes, plus extra to serve
freshly ground black pepper, to taste

TIPS: *Feel free to swap some of the dried herbs for a mixture of fresh herbs. Alternatively, you could change the flavour by using coriander, mint and parsley for a fresh taste, or oregano, basil and thyme for a Mediterranean twist.*

If you prefer thicker wedges to chips, just adjust the timing to allow for a longer cooking time.

Toasted black beans

Per serving 217 kcals | 12g fat | 1.7g saturates | 16.5g carbohydrates | 11.1g protein | 0.5g sugars

1. Preheat the oven to 220°/200°C fan/425°F/gas mark 7.

2. Pat the black beans dry with a paper towel, then place in a bowl. Add all the other ingredients and toss to coat. Lay the black beans out in an even layer on a baking tray.

3. Place in the oven for 15 minutes. Remove from the oven and stir, then return to the oven for up to 10 more minutes. Keep an eye on the beans to make sure they don't burn. They should be crisp, sizzling and lightly toasted in colour.

4. Remove from the oven and set aside for 2–3 minutes or until cool enough to the touch. Serve as a snack or as a topping to some of our soups.

SERVES 2

160g (5¾oz) canned black
  beans, drained
2 teaspoons olive oil
1 tablespoon hemp seeds
1 tablespoon pumpkin seeds
handful of freshly chopped
  coriander
pinch of sea salt and freshly
  ground black pepper, to
  taste

Spiced chickpeas

Per serving 187 kcals | 8.5g fat | 1.3g saturates | 19.1g carbohydrates | 5.8g protein | 0.9g sugars

1. Pat the chickpeas dry with a paper towel, then place in a bowl. Add the curry powder and allspice, and season with salt and pepper.

2. Heat the oil in a saucepan over a low heat and add the seasoned chickpeas. Cook for 3–4 minutes or until the chickpeas are lightly toasted and you can smell the spices.

3. Serve warm as a snack or as a topping to some of our soups.

SERVES 2

160g (5¾oz) canned
  chickpeas, drained
1 teaspoon curry powder
¼ teaspoon ground allspice
1 tablespoon olive oil
salt and freshly ground black
  pepper, to taste

Parsnip crisps

Per serving 119 kcals | 7.6g fat | 1.2g saturates | 9.3g carbohydrates | 1.5g protein | 3.9g sugars

1. Preheat the oven to 160°C/140°C fan/325°F/gas mark 3.

2. Use a mandolin or a peeler to create thin strips from the parsnips. You could also use a knife to cut the parsnip into very thin slices but do this carefully.

3. Put the oil, thyme, salt and pepper in a bowl and add the parsnip slices. Toss to coat, then lay the slices out in a single layer on a baking tray. This is very important, because if they overlap, they will steam and not crisp up. If necessary, lay them out over two trays.

4. Bake for 10 minutes. Remove from the oven and use a spatula to stir the parsnips around, then return to the oven for a further 10–15 minutes or until fully crisp.

5. Serve as a snack or as an accompaniment to some of our soup recipes.

SERVES 2

2 medium parsnips (160g/5¾oz), peeled
1 tablespoon olive oil
1 teaspoon dried thyme
pinch of sea salt
pinch of freshly ground black pepper

Crunchy sweetcorn

Per serving 91 kcals | 7.8g fat | 1.1g saturates | 2.2g carbohydrates | 2.1g protein | 1.6g sugars

1. Preheat the oven to 200°C/180°C fan/400°F/gas mark 6.

2. Mix all the ingredients together in a bowl and toss to coat the sweetcorn in the seasoning. Lay out the sweetcorn in an even layer on a baking tray.

3. Place in the oven for 15–20 minutes. Check the sweetcorn and, if necessary, cook for a further 5 minutes until lightly browned.

4. Remove from the oven and serve as a snack or a topping to some of our soups.

SERVES 2

160g (5¾oz) sweetcorn, tinned or frozen
1 tablespoon olive oil
handful of freshly chopped parsley
pinch of sweet smoked paprika
pinch of sea salt and freshly ground black pepper

Tofu egg

Per serving 205 kcals | 11g fat | 1.4g saturates | 7g carbohydrates | 17.8g protein | 1.9g sugars

1. Preheat your oven to 240°C/220°C fan/475°F/gas mark 9 and line a baking tray with baking paper.

2. Cut two thin slices from the largest area of the tofu. Using a knife or a cookie cutter, cut two large circles out of the tofu slices. Set aside.

3. In a small bowl, mix together the rest of the ingredients to create the 'yolk' and season with salt and pepper.

4. Use a smaller cookie cutter or a knife to cut out a smaller circle from the centre of the round tofu slices for the 'yolk'.

5. Place on your baking tray and fill the inner circle with the 'yolk' mixture.

6. Bake for 10 minutes and serve.

SERVES 2

200g (7oz) tofu
**3 tablespoons canned
  pumpkin purée**
1 teaspoon nutritional yeast
1 teaspoon cornflour
1 teaspoon cold water
pinch of garlic powder
¼ teaspoon maple syrup
  (optional)
1 teaspoon olive oil
pinch of sea salt and freshly
  ground black pepper, to
  taste

'Buttermilk' pancakes with blueberries

*Per serving 684 kcals | 15g fat | 1.4g saturates | 121.1g carbohydrates | 12.8g protein | 66.8g sugars
Vitamins C, B1 & B6, Folate, Potassium, Phosphorus & Manganese*

We can't think of a better way to chat, discuss, gossip and debate than with a plate of fruit-hearty pancakes ready and waiting to be devoured.

1. Place all the compote ingredients in a medium saucepan over a medium heat and simmer for 10–15 minutes, stirring frequently, until the fruit is soft and the compote looks jammy.

2. For the pancakes, create the 'buttermilk' by adding the lemon juice to the plant milk. Stir and set aside for 5 minutes. Next, mix the flaxseed with the warm water and stir. Set aside for 5 minutes.

3. Place your flour, sugar, baking powder and cinnamon in a large bowl and mix together thoroughly. Make a well in the centre of the mixture and pour in the flaxseed mixture, 'buttermilk' mixture and vanilla extract. Stir well to create a thick, smooth batter. Stir in the vegetable oil until it is combined and the batter has a smooth sheen.

4. Lightly grease a frying pan and place over a medium heat. Once hot, reduce the heat to low and add 2 tablespoons of batter to the pan. Dot with 15g (½oz) dried blueberries.

5. Cook for 1–2 minutes, or until you can slide a spatula all the way underneath the pancake. Then flip and cook for about 1 minute on the other side. Repeat with the remaining batter.

6. Divide the pancakes between three plates and serve topped with the compote and chopped banana, along with a 150ml (¼ pint) glass of orange juice per person.

SERVES 3

For the pancake batter
2 teaspoons lemon juice
175ml (6floz) plant milk
1 tablespoon ground flaxseed
3 tablespoons warm water
185g (6½oz) plain flour
1 tablespoon granulated sugar
1 tablespoon baking powder
1 teaspoon ground cinnamon
½ teaspoon vanilla extract
2 tablespoons vegetable oil,
  plus more for greasing
90g (3¼oz) dried blueberries

For the berry compote
240g (8½oz) raspberries, fresh
  or frozen
240g (8½oz) eating apples,
  peeled, cored and chopped
1 tablespoon maple syrup
75ml (2½floz) water

To serve
3 bananas (240g), sliced
450ml (16floz) orange juice

TIP: *If you're using gluten-free flour, add ½ teaspoon xanthan gum to the batter unless your flour already contains it.*

Rainbow tart

Per serving 570 kcals | 25g fat | 9.3g saturates | 68.2g carbohydrates | 9.2g protein | 31.5g sugars
Vitamins A & C, Folate & Potassium

This tart makes a lovely display and is a great way of using up any leftover vegetables. We recently served these at a family wedding and received loads of compliments. This tart provides all of your 5 a day for two people, as the chutney provides 2 of your 5!

1. Preheat the oven to 210°C/190°C fan/410°F/gas mark 6½. Use a mandolin, a wide-bladed peeler or a small sharp knife to cut the carrots, courgettes and aubergine into long, thin strips.

2. Roll out the pastry and line a 20-cm (8-inch) tartlet case. Spread the chutney over the base of the pastry case, then sprinkle over the vegan salad cheese (if using).

3. Lay out all the carrot strips, one on top of the other. Now, curl the whole bundle into a tight spiral. Place in the centre of the pastry case. Take the strips of courgette and one at a time, arrange the courgettes around the carrots to continue the spiral outwards. Do the same with the aubergine strips until the vegetables reach the outer crust of the pastry dish.

4. Use a pastry brush to dab the tops of the vegetables with the olive oil.

5. Bake for 35–40 minutes. Use a sharp knife to check if the carrots have fully softened. If the tart needs further cooking but is starting to brown on top, cover with a layer of tin foil and cook for a further 10 minutes or until the vegetables are soft.

6. Remove from the oven and serve warm. Enjoy!

SERVES 2

2 medium carrots (160g/5¾oz), peeled and trimmed

1 courgette (160g/5¾oz), trimmed

1–2 medium aubergines (160g/5¾oz), trimmed

280g (10oz) vegan shortcrust pastry

70g (2½oz) feta-style vegan salad cheese (optional)

1 batch red onion chutney (page 118)

2 teaspoons olive oil

TIP: *If you want to serve 4, or save some for later, cut the tart into quarters and serve with a tossed salad or sweet potato fries (page 123).*

Black bean burritos with avocado salsa

Per serving 709 kcals | 37g fat | 5.9g saturates | 71.6g carbohydrates | 16.7g protein | 17.9g sugars
Vitamins A, C, E, B1 & B6, Folate, Potassium, Phosphorus, Copper & Manganese

You can never go wrong with burritos and avocados!
This will provide your 5 a day – or 6 a day if you serve it
with our sweet potato fries on page 123 – in one healthy,
filling and nutritious meal that is sure to keep you going!

1. Preheat the oven to 220°C/200°C fan/425°F/gas mark 7.

2. Lay out the sweet potatoes on a baking tray and
drizzle with 1 tablespoon of the oil. Season with salt and
pepper, then stir to coat completely. Place in the oven
for 20–25 minutes or until fully cooked and crispy at the
edges. Set aside, but keep the oven on.

3. Meanwhile, heat the remaining oil in a medium-sized
saucepan over a low heat. Add the onions and cook
for 5–10 minutes, or until starting to caramelize. Add
the black beans and sweetcorn, then season. Cook for
a further 5–6 minutes, stirring frequently and lightly
mashing the beans with your spoon. Set aside.

4. For the salsa, place all the ingredients in a food
processor and blend until smooth. Season to taste, then
set aside while you finish the rest of the dish.

5. Lay out the tortillas and divide the black bean mixture
between them. Top with the roasted sweet potatoes,
then sprinkle over the cheese, if using. Wrap up the
tortillas, then place them in a small baking tray or dish so
that they are bunched up together and stay closed. Place
back in the oven for 5–10 minutes or until the tortillas
become crisp and their edges are slightly browned.

6. Divide the burritos between two plates and serve
topped with the avocado salsa.

SERVES 2

1 medium sweet potato
   (160g/5¾oz), peeled and
   chopped
2 tablespoons vegetable oil
2 medium red onions
   (160g/5¾oz), chopped
160g (5¾oz) canned black
   beans, drained
160g (5¾oz) sweetcorn, frozen
   or canned
4 tortilla wraps
150g (5½oz) vegan Cheddar-
   style cheese (optional)
salt and freshly ground black
   pepper, to taste

For the avocado salsa:
300g (10½oz) tomato salsa
handful of freshly chopped
   mint
handful of freshly chopped
   coriander
2 avocados (160g/5¾oz),
   peeled, pitted and roughly
   chopped
juice of 1 lime
1 garlic clove, crushed

Rainbow lasagne

Per serving 219 kcals | 10g fat | 1.2g saturates | 19.1g carbohydrates | 6.9g protein | 16g sugars
Vitamins C, B1 & B6, Folate & Potassium

This recipe requires a bit more work than the other dishes featured in this book, but the results are more than worth it! Nothing beats cutting into the lasagne to unveil the rainbow colours. Use a deep lasagne dish!

1. Preheat the oven to 220°C/200°C fan/425°F/gas mark 7.

2. Lay the butternut squash out on a baking tray. Drizzle over the oil, sprinkle over the nutmeg and season with salt and pepper and mix until the cubes are fully coated. Roast for 20 minutes, then sprinkle over the garlic and return to the oven for another 10 minutes. Set aside.

3. Once cool, use a hand blender to blend the butternut squash into a purée. Set aside until needed.

4. Meanwhile, for the mushroom layer, heat the oil in a medium-sized pan over a low heat, then add the mushrooms. Cook for 5–7 minutes, stirring regularly. Once the mushroom juices have evaporated, add the thyme and season with salt and pepper. Cook for a further 1–2 minutes. Transfer to a bowl and set aside.

5. For the tomato sauce, heat the oil in the pan over a low heat. Add the onions and garlic. Cook, stirring, for 5–7 minutes. Add the basil and season with salt and pepper. When the onions start to caramelize, pour in the tomatoes. Increase the heat and bring to the boil, then reduce the heat to low for a further 3–4 minutes, stirring occasionally. Taste for seasoning, then set aside.

6. For the beetroot layer, blend the beetroot, thyme and salt in a blender until the mixture is fairly smooth but

SERVES 4

For the butternut squash layer:
½ butternut squash (320g/11½oz), peeled and chopped
1½ tablespoons vegetable oil
1 teaspoon ground nutmeg
2 garlic cloves, finely chopped
salt and freshly ground black pepper, to taste

For the mushroom layer:
1 tablespoon vegetable oil
320g (11½oz) chestnut mushrooms, sliced
1 teaspoon fresh thyme leaves

For the tomato sauce:
1 tablespoon vegetable oil
4 medium onions (320g/11½oz), chopped
2 garlic cloves, finely chopped
large handful of fresh basil, roughly chopped
400g (14oz) canned tomatoes

For the beetroot layer:
320g (11½oz) vacuum-packed
  beetroot, drained
2 teaspoons dried thyme
pinch of salt
50g (1¾oz) vegan cheese,
  grated

For the béchamel sauce:
25g (1oz) margarine, plus extra
  for greasing the dish
25g (1oz) plain flour, or 2
  tablespoons rice/potato flour
½ teaspoon ground nutmeg
250ml (9floz) plant milk,
  unsweetened
100g (3½oz) vegan cheese,
  grated

dried or fresh lasagne sheets
  (plain or verde)

some small chunks remain. Tip into a clean bowl and stir in your vegan cheese.

7. Lastly, make the béchamel sauce. In a small saucepan, melt the margarine over a low heat, then add the flour and nutmeg. Whisk the flour and margarine so that they come together in a sticky clump. Pour in about a quarter of the plant milk and whisk until the béchamel begins to look like thick mashed potato. Keep adding the milk, a little at a time, continuously whisking. Once all the milk is in and the sauce is as smooth as possible, keep whisking for another 30 seconds, then remove from the heat. Stir in the vegan cheese and season with salt and pepper.

8. Reduce the oven heat to 190°C/170°C fan/375°F/gas mark 3. Grease your deep lasagne dish with margarine, then arrange one layer of lasagne sheets in the bottom. Pour in the tomato sauce, and top with another layer of lasagne sheets. Now spread on the beetroot layer and top with another layer of lasagne sheets. Next add the butternut squash layer and top with another layer of lasagne sheets. Now add the sautéed mushrooms. Add a final layer of lasagne sheets, then pour the béchamel sauce over the top and sprinkle over the cheese.

9. Place in the oven for 25 minutes, or until the top is golden brown.

10. Cut into four slices, then serve. Eat it all at once for a large dinner or split into smaller pieces to have your 5 a day over lunch and dinner.

Herby pie

Per serving 794 kcals | 39g fat | 11g saturates | 77.2g carbohydrates | 21.8g protein | 25.8g sugars
Vitamins A, C, B1 & B6, Folate, Potassium, Phosphorus, Zinc & Manganese

The key to this dish is in the sumptuous, silky white sauce, which is a doddle to make. Once you've got the hang of this pie, you can change things up a little and try out different veg. If, like us, you like to eat and cook with the seasons, our seasonality chart on page 11 might nudge you in the right direction for some inspiration.

1. Preheat the oven to 200°C/180°C fan/400°F/gas mark 6.

2. Heat the oil in a large saucepan over a low heat. Add all the vegetables. Cook for 1 minute, then add the garlic, herbs and 'chicken' (if using). Season with salt and pepper and cook for about 10 minutes more, stirring regularly, until the onions are translucent and the carrots and parsnips are slightly soft when pierced with a fork.

3. Meanwhile, in a medium saucepan, melt the margarine over a low heat. Whisk in the flour. Pour in the vegetable stock, plant milk, parsley and nutmeg. Season with salt and pepper. Keep whisking until the sauce begins to thicken and coats the back of a spoon.

4. Pour the sauce over the cooked vegetables and stir to combine. Take off the heat and leave to cool to room temperature for about 20 minutes Divide your pastry into two pieces, one twice as large as the other. Roll out the larger piece to a thickness of 3mm (1⅛ inches) and use it to line the base and sides of a 23-cm (9-inch) pie dish, letting the excess pastry overhang.

5. Pour the filling into the pastry case. Roll out the remaining pastry to make the lid. Using a pastry brush, dab a little plant milk all around the edge of the exposed pastry in the dish – to help seal the edges.

SERVES 2

1 tablespoon olive oil
2 medium onions, (160g/5¾oz), diced
160g (5¾oz) sweetcorn, fresh, tinned or frozen
2 medium carrots (160g/5¾oz), peeled and diced
2 medium parsnips (160g/5¾oz), peeled and diced
160g (5¾oz) green beans, cut into chunks
2 garlic cloves, minced
1 teaspoon dried oregano
½ teaspoon dried sage
100g (3½oz) vegan 'chicken' pieces (optional)
50g (1¾oz) margarine
50g (1¾oz) flour
350ml (12floz) vegetable stock
200ml (7floz) plant milk, plus extra
1 teaspoon dried parsley
pinch of nutmeg
350g (12oz) premade/shop-bought shortcrust pastry, at room temperature
salt and freshly ground black pepper, to taste

6. Carefully lay the pastry lid over the pie. Use a knife to cut off any excess pastry all the way around the dish. Finally, brush the top of the pie with a bit more plant milk. Score a small 'X' in the middle of the pie to allow steam to escape.

7. Bake for 25–30 minutes or until the pastry is cooked through and the top of the pie is golden-brown. When cooked, remove from the oven and let sit for 5 minutes before serving. Cut into quarters to allow for two servings per person split between lunch and dinner.

Index

Resources

More information on 5 a day guidelines
- World Health Organization (www.who.int)

Stockists of Soupologie 5 a day soups
- *Ocado* (www.ocado.com)
- *Waitrose* (www.waitrose.com)
- *Whole Foods* (www.wholefoodsmarket.com)
- *Planet Organic* (www.planetorganic.com)
- *Carrefour* (www.carrefour.com)
- *As Nature Intended*
- *Soupologie* (www.soupologie.com)
- *Many independent retailers*

Soupologie
www.soupologie.com
@soupologie

About Soupologie

Soupologie began from a place of passion and heart-felt belief that soup should taste – and make you feel – great. Everything we do comes from that initial starting point.

In the early days, Stephen, making sure that his kids ate their vegetables in the most effortless way possible, through colourful plant-based soups! That turned into making soup for others, in the knowledge that the power and goodness of eating whole vegetables and fruits is best done as part of a delicious and comforting, often shared, experience. And so, it happened that we found ourselves at a Christmas market in 2011, serving up Stephen's delicious plant-based soups to an enthusiastic crowd who were the inspiration behind the founding of Soupologie.

The passion and ethos that drove us then still drives us today, as the only family-run soup company around. Reinventing soup from being a basic staple into a fundamental part of a healthy diet has been our mission over the years. We want to create flavoursome bowls of warming nourishment that transform the image of soup forever. We want to turn the mundane into the magnificent, from that first tempting glimpse of rich velvety smoothness to the final satisfied scraping of the bowl. Sheer moments of joy! In our minds, the perfect bowl of soup will reach deep within you, stirring comforting memories of warmer places and smiling faces. Wherever your own happy place exists, that's where we want our soup to transport you. And whilst there, the perfect soup will nurture and fuel your body with its nutrients and goodness. Lofty ambitions indeed. Humble bowl of soup, be humble no more!

Our ready-made soups, available from our website and other retailers, are all vegan and free from the 14 main allergens. We want as many people as possible to be able to enjoy them, and we have never felt the need to add thickeners like cornflour, or use palm oil, or add sugar. We let the plants and our cooking do the talking, keeping it simple and using ingredients that most of us can find in our kitchen.

With the expansion of our range into vegan broths with added vitamin D and highly nutritious ready meals, we look forward to welcoming you into the Soupologie family. Come and say 'hi' to us if you see us in store at one of our samplings or tag us @soupologie in your photos on social media - we always love seeing what you're up to, particularly if it involves one of our soups!

Acknowledgements

This book would never have come to fruition without my parents, Amanda & Stephen. They are the founders of Soupologie and my source of support, love & guidance. I want to thank my best friends, my sisters: Fredericka, Victoria & Henrietta, along with my brothers-in-law, Jeremy & Daniel.

My family were forced to sample more soups than they were quite frankly comfortable with, but they are always honest and have made me a better cook as a result. A special mention goes to my dogs, who were lying at my feet the whole way through writing this book.

A huge thanks goes to Ren Bhojoo for her tremendous help and patience. I am very grateful to my agent, Amanda Preston, and the whole team at Kyle Books, especially Isabel and Judith, for their help, support & encouragement.

Finally, I would like to thank Soupologistas everywhere whose continued support means the world. We'd love you to tag us @soupologie on our social media with all your delicious dishes!

An Hachette UK Company
www.hachette.co.uk

First published in Great Britain in 2020 by
Kyle Books, an imprint of Kyle Cathie Ltd
Carmelite House
50 Victoria Embankment
London EC4Y 0DY
www.kylebooks.co.uk

ISBN: 978 0 85783 8810

Text copyright 2020 © Anastasia Argent
Design and layout copyright 2020 © Kyle Cathie Ltd

Distributed in the US by Hachette Book Group,
1290 Avenue of the Americas,
4th and 5th Floors, New York, NY 10104

Distributed in Canada by Canadian Manda Group,
664 Annette St., Toronto, Ontario, Canada M6S 2C8

Anastasia Argent is hereby identified as the author of this work in
accordance with Section 77 of the Copyright, Designs and Patents
Act 1988.

All rights reserved. No part of this work may be reproduced or utilized
in any form or by any means, electronic or mechanical, including
photocopying, recording or by any information storage and retrieval
system, without the prior written permission of the publisher.

Editorial Director: Judith Hannam
Publisher: Joanna Copestick
Editor: Isabel Gonzalez-Prendergast
Photography: Tamin Jones
Food styling: Lizzie Harris
Props styling: Rachel Vere
Cover & chapter opener design: Nikki Ellis
Illustrations: Hannah Meur
Production: Katherine Hockley

A Cataloguing in Publication record for this title is available from
the British Library

Printed and bound in China

10 9 8 7 6 5 4 3 2 1